Let's Ask Michael

The McGraw·Hill Companies

Cataloging-in-Publication Data is on file with the Library of Congress.

1 2 3 4 5 6 7 8 9 0   DOC/DOC 0 9 8 7 6 5 4 3

ISBN 0-07-141627-7

The sponsoring editor for this book was Cary Sullivan and the production supervisor was Sherri Souffiance. This book was set in Helvetica.

Book designed by Juston Payne Design.

All photographs by Michael Payne unless otherwise stated.

Printed and bound by RR Donnelley.

This book was printed on acid-free paper.

McGraw-Hill books are available at special quantity discounts to use as premiums and sales promotions, or for use in corporate training programs. For more information, please write to the Director of Special Sales, Professional Publishing, McGraw-Hill, Two Penn Plaza, New York, NY 10121-2298. Or contact your local bookstore.

LET'S ASK MICHAEL

100 Practical Solutions for Design Challenges

A Book By
Michael Payne

Host and Interior Designer
of Home and Garden Television's popular show,
Designing for the Sexes

McGraw-Hill

New York   Chicago   San Francisco   Lisbon   London
Madrid   Mexico City   Milan   New Delhi   San Juan
Seoul   Singapore   Sydney   Toronto

To Lionel and Mary Payne

whose love and dedication to their home inspired me to pursue a life of design

ACKNOWLEDGMENTS

During the writing and production of "Let's Ask Michael," I received help and support from many others, which was invaluable in making the book come together. I would like to thank my dear friends Liz and David Kirschner for generously opening up their home to me so that photographs could be taken to illustrate certain points. I would also like to thank the clients who allowed me to return (long after project completion) to photograph the project for illustrative purposes in this book:

Donick and Kim Cary
William Cobert and Diane O'Connor
Ray and Maryann Costa
Ed and Carol Felman

Diana and Steve Marcus
Paul and Jackie Pepperman
Kathy and Jim Wehri
Bill and Barbara Zimmerman

Special thanks also go to Bill Dow for accompanying me in photographing some of these homes.

I am very grateful to all the other "Designing For the Sexes" clients, as well as my private clients, whose homes have been featured in this book:

Rob and Joan Blackman
Christopher and Tonya Eggleston
Frank and Andrea Epinger
Peter and Gail Field
Daniel and Jeri Floyd
Robert and Ava Gold
Dana Graham and Lianne La Reine
John and Molly Gray
Robert and Carol Haymer
John and Elizabeth Hrovat
Ron and LM Jobson
Bill Kane and Cindy Dole
Fred and Sheila Kerz
Michael and Sharon Landau
Carol La Porta
Chris Williams and Steve Luce
Neil and Andrea Miller

Rick and Giselle Page
Dave and April Rossi
Rich Ruttenberg and Susan Marder
Bob and Yvonne Sherman
Victor Sherman
Josh and Ruth Silver
Greg and Eileen Smith
Dave and Jan Spivey
Dom and Gloria Stasi
Loren Stephens
Mark and Janine Stern
Kent and Joanne Takemoto
Jay and Lori Telenda
Larry and Maureen Varnes
Larry and Ann Wallace
Frank and Debbie Winton

Thanks to Sheri Hirschfeld from Ann Sachs and Stephen from Elijah Slocum for welcoming us to their showrooms and allowing us to capture their beautiful inventory.

Thanks to everyone at McGraw-Hill who helped make this book a reality, particularly Cary Sullivan, for without her dedication from inception to completion, this book would not exist today.

Finally, I would like to thank the graphic designer, my son Juston, for creatively putting the book together and my wife, Janice, whose hard work, rational criticism, and sage advice played a critical role in this whole endeavor.

professional interior design

INTRODUCTION

Let me tell you a true story. A couple who watch my television show, "Designing For The Sexes," emailed me about a year ago, saying they had a very heated discussion about a design disagreement in their home. In frustration, and not being able to resolve their conflict themselves, the husband finally exclaimed, "Let's ask Michael." When I read the email I immediately thought it could be a perfect basis for a book.

I have received an ever-increasing stream of email since "Designing For The Sexes" first aired on HGTV on October 1, 1998. Many emails merely comment on the show, but just as many include questions about design issues. Many of the design questions have a similar basis and universal appeal. I therefore decided to take some of the most frequently asked questions -- as well as some of the more entertaining ones -- along with my answers, and publish them in a book. In some cases, if the question was too specific to a particular home, I took the liberty of modifying the question in order to make it more useful for a general audience. Additionally, my original email answers did not include photographs, so I have modified them in order to incorporate photographs or graphic representations for a visual reference.

As you read the questions and then my answers, you will likely realize that my underlying design philosophy is that all spaces in a home should reflect the resident's needs as well as personality. Rooms are like machines. Before any thought is given to their appearance, they need to work. Whether it is a kitchen, a den, or a bedroom, the function is paramount. It is only after a successful design is formulated that the decorative aspects become important. Should the room be contemporary, traditional, retro, or eclectic? Only the homeowners -- the people who reside in the space -- can decide what makes them comfortable and happy. Some people love bold colors, while others enjoy the subtlety of whites and neutral. There really are no "rights" or "wrongs". There are merely combinations of an almost infinite number of variables, with some that work better together than others, either from a practical or an aesthetic standpoint.

Another design philosophy to which I have adhered throughout my career involves three fundamental facts, all of which are important to remember if you work with an interior designer:
1) Never forget whose home it is
2) Never forget whose money is being spent
3) Never forget who will be living in the home after the designer is long gone

Interior design is all about you. Do whatever it takes to give yourself a home that functions the way you want it to, and that looks and feels like your personal refuge. To accomplish this sometimes daunting task, you will likely have to overcome issues such as too many choices, too little knowledge, and dissenting opinions among members of the household. Hopefully this book will guide you through successful resolutions to some design trials and tribulations of your own, and offer the comforting knowledge that you are not alone in facing design challenges!

I hope you enjoy *Let's Ask Michael*, and that you find the solutions you are looking for.

www.michaelpayne.com

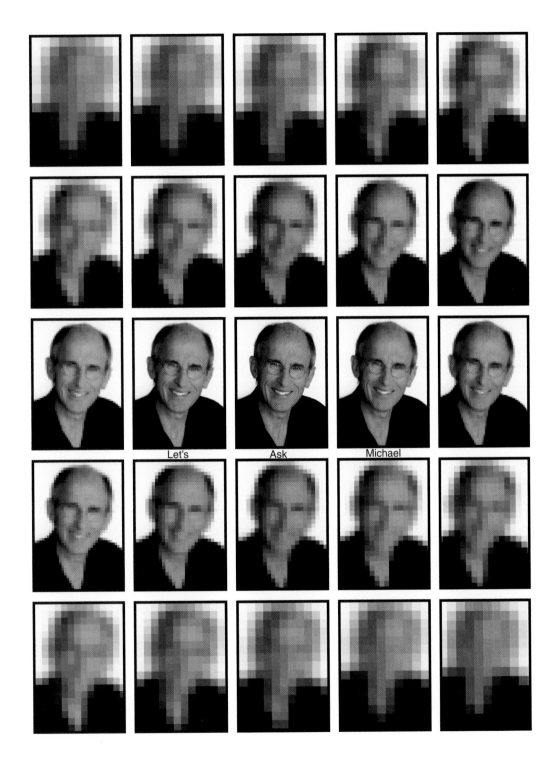

Let's   Ask   Michael

Chapter 1
the bedroom

We spend more time in the bedroom than any other room, yet are conscious during very little of it. It is often a space of great dissension between couples because everyone has a different idea of what a bedroom should be. Many favor the maximum comfort, while others think it should be more of a showplace.

People are particularly finicky about the colors and materials used in the bedroom, and often favor solutions that feel soft and light. To many, an unappealing bedroom would be one in which they wake up, step on a cold floor, and look around at a boring room. Most people want warmth and personality, but have trouble translating that into a design. After all, there are many means of achieving warmth, but with so many choices, people often feel overwhelmed and cannot decide on anything. This chapter answers questions, solves common design dilemmas, and presents plenty of options for achieving beautifully decorated bedrooms.

D ear Michael,

My wife and I are in the process of redoing our master bedroom, and are considering opening the ceiling. What are the advantages of doing this, and should we be mindful to fill the space with different types of furniture? I'm worried opening it will create a completely different feeling in the room that will make our old furniture look out of place.

Charlie and Fanny
Wilmington, DE

Opening up the ceiling dramatically affects the occupant's experience in the room. Most people live in a world of ceiling heights between 8 and 9 feet, so one's spirits positively soar upon entering a cathedral, hotel atrium, airport terminal, or other space with lofty ceilings of 50 feet or more. In a home, ceilings of approximately 20 feet or more are becoming increasingly popular.

High ceilings in the home present new challenges. Maintaining a consistent temperature in a room with high ceilings presents a difficulty because you risk heating the ceiling rafters instead of your feet. Fans do an excellent job of keeping the air circulating, as do vents in both the ceiling and floor.

Effectively lighting large spaces often requires utilization of nearly every form of lighting appliance. Recessed lighting can be used whether the ceiling is flat or angled, but is not terribly cozy, and it also creates a large amount of glare. A chandelier can work beautifully, as it will cast light up onto the ceiling as well as fill the room with light, and bedside table lamps are crucial for filling the room out with light. Dedicated picture lights are typically the best means of illuminating art. All lights in the room should be on individual dimmers.

The scale of your existing furniture needs careful consideration. The volume of your room will have substantially increased, and your furniture needs to be in step. Draperies can also be hung higher and have a more full quality.

The beautiful bedroom pictured at left is a fine example of scale. The soaring ceiling amplified by the heavy, hand-hewn beams creates a volume more cozy than cavernous. The tall four poster bed fits perfectly in the space, as do the towering carved display cabinet, the large leather chair, ottoman, and huge mirror. The impersonal feeling large rooms often impart can be diminished by countering size with size.

Dear Michael,

My husband and I recently repainted our bedroom, and we even bought all new furniture for it. We truly couldn't be happier with the final product, which is actually the cause of our problem! I want to spend more time in it when I am at home, but can't really find a reason to. I want a comfortable place to relax and read a book, but do not want to install a desk. Is there another option for adding some seating to the room that will not make it feel like an office but will provide a place to sit around and relax?

Teresa

Los Angeles, CA

Nothing is more important than being comfortable in your own bedroom. Don't be afraid to set up tables with collections that may take up floor space but please you every time you walk into the room.

A comfortable lounge chair or chaise would be a wonderful addition to your bedroom. Not only will it soften the room's appearance, but it will also provide a supremely comfortable place to read and enjoy the tranquility of your new room. You should pick the most comfortable, most beautiful, most appealing chair you can find so that it will continually beckon you. If your space is limited, this should not be a problem because there are many beautiful, small lounge chairs. Make sure your upholstery fabric is striking and coordinates with your wall color.

D ear Michael,

We live in a condo, and while some of the rooms are well proportioned and closet space is ample, we desperately need additional storage space in our master bedroom. We would like to know what would be the best way to maximize storage and include a television and components. We want to integrate them into the room without overwhelming the space.

Katie and Alex
Philadelphia, PA

Space optimization becomes critical when dealing with confined spaces such as apartments and condos. When designing for such environments, I take inspiration from a place I used to live: a boat. In a boat, you need to make every inch count. In your bedroom, ottomans can be coffee tables with storage inside a hinged top, beds can have storage drawers for bulky items underneath, and television cabinets can act as supplementary dressers. I recommend installing wall cabinets with striking hardware as functional art pieces. Remember -- a place for everything and everything in its right place.

Consider having custom built-in cabinetry along one of the walls, preferably the one facing the bed. The television and components can disap-
pear completely behind pocket doors in a center section. Along either
side, you can have closed lower cabinetry both below and above for additional storage. The counter space in between the upper and lower cabinets can be used for display and functions to visually break-up the block
of cabinetry. Use under cabinet lighting to highlight display items and to
cast a glow on the counter surface.

In this photo, the cabinetry is painted in a semi-gloss finish to match and
coordinate with the trim in the room. With the wall color in a flat finish, a
nice contrast is created between the two colors and finishes. This example is both a functional and aesthetic solution to satisfy your storage
requirements.

Dear Michael,

Here's a simple question with, at least in my opinion, a not-so-simple answer. I have one TV, but want to watch it from different seating positions in my bedroom. Is an ugly Lazy Susan the only way to go?

Monty and Yasmine
Erie, PA

You might be surprised to learn how common this problem is. Often in a bedroom you want to watch television from a seating area and from bed. Putting the television on a pull-out and swivel tray in a cabinet is the best solution. In the photographs below is a custom solution I designed to give a swiveling television in a space too small to accommodate a cabinet. It called for a contemporary, minimalist design, and allows viewing from a wide range of directions.

ear Michael,

I'm redoing my guest room on a tight budget, but don't want it to come off as being completely bland. I have a colorful painting to hang, and am worried any wall color aside from white will conflict with it. What should I do?

Sara
Billings, MT

I would choose a color that you enjoy in the painting you intend to hang, and then match your walls to that color. You will be amazed at how that color in the painting leaps out when surrounded by it on the walls. The fram-ing and matting of your painting is important as well because it serves as a buffer that prevents conflict between the wall color and the other colors in the painting. If you have any doubt about art's being hung on bold color walls, a trip to the Getty Museum in Los Angeles will allay your fears. There are deep blue, red, gray, and yellow walls, and paintings look marvelous. Pick a color in your art, and paint your walls and choose your bedding and drapery fabrics according to this choice.

Dear Michael,

My husband and I have just moved into a new home, and we have a bumped-out bay window in our bedroom. I am looking for window treatments for our room more for looks than functional reasons, but I'm stumped. My husband wants vertical blinds, but I can't stand them. We do not need to draw the blinds for privacy, but we find the unadorned windows to be incredibly boring.

Do you have any suggestions? We'd love to hear from you.

Shari
Chicago, IL

If you need to be able to close the draperies for light control, I would consider a rod and rings approach. Each section of the bay will have its own rod and rings, with the left window's draperies stacking on the left, and

the right window's draperies stacking on the right. The center section will have two draperies, half stacking on the left and the other half on the right, leaving four panels when the draperies are open.

If you have no need to close the draperies, and it sounds like you do not, you can just swag the draperies fabric over the three rods and have two rod-to-floor panels at the end framing the bay opening. Choose an appropriate color so the fabric works well with your color scheme and adds a distinct element to the overall look.

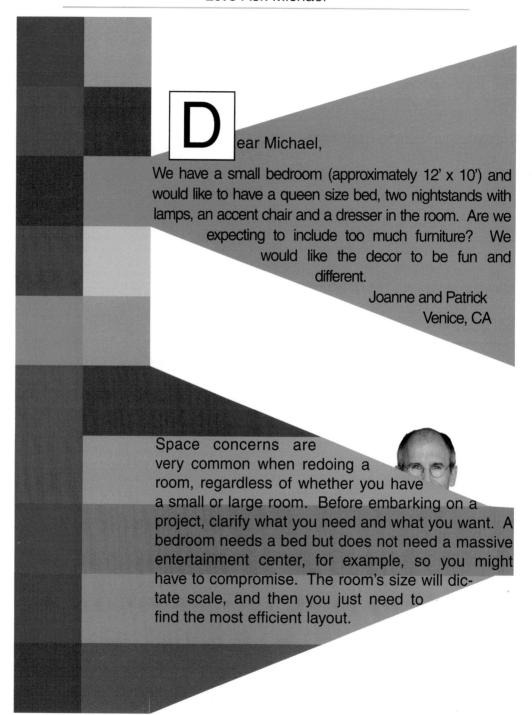

D

ear Michael,

We have a small bedroom (approximately 12' x 10') and would like to have a queen size bed, two nightstands with lamps, an accent chair and a dresser in the room. Are we expecting to include too much furniture? We would like the decor to be fun and different.

Joanne and Patrick
Venice, CA

Space concerns are very common when redoing a room, regardless of whether you have a small or large room. Before embarking on a project, clarify what you need and what you want. A bedroom needs a bed but does not need a massive entertainment center, for example, so you might have to compromise. The room's size will dictate scale, and then you just need to find the most efficient layout.

If your furniture is not too large, try positioning the bed at a 45° angle to add a visually exciting element to the room. Make sure you have an interesting headboard because it will be a focal point. You will have space behind the headboard for a screen, a plant, or a triangular table for decorative accessories.

Find some fun fabrics for the bedding ensemble and use decorative throw pillows for accents. Paint the walls a strong color for drama and contrast, choosing one of the colors from your bedding as inspiration. Also, consider swing arm wall mounted lamps if table lamps feel too crowded on the nightstands.

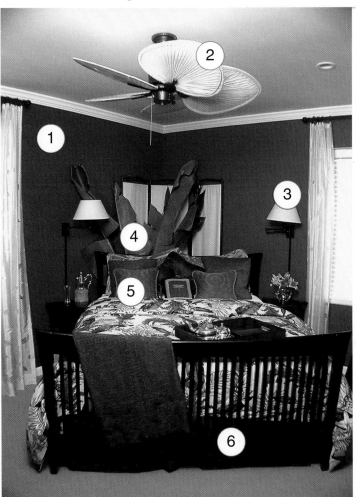

1. The strong red color creates a dramatic backdrop to the exotic tropical scheme.

2. This fan with its leaf-like blades is perfectly consistent with the theme.

3. Wall-mounted lamps save floor and bed-stand space. Both the white shade and wrought iron fixture contrast nicely with the wall color.

4. The palm adds visual drama and contrasts beautifully with the red walls.

5. The bedding provides inspiration for the colors and theme of the room.

6. The bed set on an angle instantly makes a strong and exciting visual statement.

Dear Michael,

We are undertaking a fairly massive master bedroom remodel, and would like your input on the color scheme for the entire room. We have a large bedroom space, and then a lot more space that we have literally no idea what to do with. Right now we have a chair sitting in it. No one, except the cat, ever sits in that chair.

So the question is what do we do with that space, and what colors do we use for the room? Since it is so large, we do not want anything that will seem smothering. We definitely don't want all white, or anything too vibrant either. I tend to lean toward shades of beige, but might want to push that a little into something a bit more unique.

Lourdes and Octavio
Santa Barbara, CA

The most unique large bedroom space I ever created was for a husband and wife who were both avid basketball fans. Beyond painting their room around their team's colors, I actually installed a miniature basketball court against one wall! With a polished wood floor, team graphic, and a slightly scaled-down hoop, they could play one on one without leaving their room.

Your bedroom sounds nearly identical to the one I worked on during another project. In the large, white bedroom pictured above and below there is a spare space that was used as a workout facility. There is, I might point out, also a chair in the space. The trouble with this room was a lack of cohesion among the various pieces. The cabinet was too separate and too contrasting from the other pieces and the wall color. Also, there was simply too much open space, making the room feel like an empty warehouse.

I suggest you consider this bonus space for one of several activities. The most attractive is to create a peaceful, private retreat where you can rest and relax, away from the rest of the house. With plush, comfortable seating, you can read, watch TV, or listen to music all within the confines of your master bedroom. I have had clients with treadmills in such spaces, in which cases I hide them behind screens. The screen in the bedroom pictured below conceals a treadmill. Other clients have used such extra spaces for yoga, meditation, and even dancing.

Regarding the room's color, find a fabric you love that can be used for the bedding or upholstery and play off those colors. If you are particularly fond of beige but would like to add a unique flare, consider golden tones. If you want a rich but easy feel, introduce both vibrant and deep reds. Greens of the same hue but different values can add a spice to the scheme. Find your ideal fabric and the room will follow.

Dear Michael,

My wife and I have a large bedroom display cabinet that houses some of our collections. She insists its lighting is perfectly adequate from our large windows, and there is no reason we should spend money on what she calls "fancy inside fluff." I am of the mind our collections will only look better with dedicated internal lighting. Can you lend any weight to either side of the debate?

Rod and Barbara
Grand Island, NE

There is not a clear answer to your seemingly straightforward question, because while daylight should be ample so long as the sun is up, lighting is imperative at night if you want to highlight your collections. Cabinet lighting is quite diverse, so you must find the best solution for both your needs and your budget. There can be small, often recessed, lights in the top of the cabinet which, if the shelves are glass, will illuminate the interior. This method becomes less viable with increased cabinet height. Another approach is to run hidden lights vertically along the sides and frame of the cabinet. The advantage of this is that all of the shelves are lit. In the case your shelves are wood, lights can be mounted under each level. Your ability to retrofit your existing cabinet will decide the best approach.

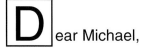ear Michael,

I'm a big pottery collector and have a fairly substantial collection. The downside of this is that I have pieces everywhere, and my husband says he's sick of the clutter. I also have had the misfortune of having several items broken by an excited dog or an overzealous child.

Ann
Burlington, VT

Here is a chance to kill two birds with one stone. You need to control your clutter by taking your collection and displaying it in a closed cabinet (*left*). It actually looks more special behind glass doors and, of course, your husband will appreciate the containment. Naturally, it will be protected from the packs of wild dogs and children running rampant in your home. You could also create some lighted alcoves where special pieces are highlighted (*below).*

D ear Michael,

I have an iron bed that does not exactly scream "feminine." I'm going to put it into my bedroom, but am worried that it will look too cold and hard. Is there a good way to soften the look of it?

Rachel

Anaheim, CA

You need not worry too much about the bed's frame because it can easily be incorporated into a soft, warm room. You should begin with picking a wall color that you believe exudes the warmth you desire. In my experience, people often gravitate to light reds for their warm quality. Once you have your wall color picked, buy a multitude of throw pillows with different colors and patterns that all coordinate with each other. I suggest hanging a large, focal piece of art to add another dimension of color, and you can use this as inspiration for the color of the throw pillows. Placing plants around the room will further counterbalance the lifeless iron. Add an area rug, and nobody will notice the relatively cold bed in such a warm room.

D|ear Michael,

My husband and I are burdened by the struggle between the battle of floral patterns. We bought a beautiful duvet that had an extremely intricate rose pattern for a bed sitting atop a rug with an ornate flower print. Let's just say that was one of the greatest catastrophes of interior design in recent times. The colors clashed, the patterns conflicted, the thorns of each metaphorically tore each other apart. My question, if you haven't guessed, is this -- can I have two different flower patterns on two different pieces as significant as a duvet and area rug, or should I just go for a solid color on one of them? The goal, of course, is to avoid any more costly battles of the patterns.

Meryl and Howie
Colorado Springs, CO

There is, unfortunately, no simple answer to your question. Beauty is subjective, and I am typically cautious when it comes to mixing complex patterns, particularly if they are as adjacent as you make them sound in your bedroom. I prefer to see such complex florals displayed on a solid ground, or on a rug with a small geometric check or stripe pattern. Often I will have highly decorative pillows on a solid sofa or bed spread, thereby minimizing competition between the fabrics. I use similarly complicated patterns on draperies because more than likely, they will be hanging against plain painted walls or, perhaps, stripes. Area rugs are a further consideration. I view them more as art than decorative accessories, but also find the colors and design of an area rug play an important role in the room. Often the rug is a powerful visual element and it is imperative all the other fabrics in the room harmonize with it. It is as though each of the various fabrics with its own pattern and coloration is an instrument in an orchestra, where each has a unique quality but also works well with the others. To continue the analogy, it sounds as though your duvet and area rug are playing different tunes. I suggest you consider a new duvet that is patterned, but also follows the lead of the rug.

chapter 2

the bathroom

The master bathroom is a unique space in that there is an equal need for utility and comfort. On the one hand, bathrooms must be durable spaces that can withstand dowsing from sinks, showers, and bathtubs, splattering of lotions and oils, and unexpected introductions of dirt from a child who played a bit too much in the mud. On the other hand, bathrooms must be warm, comfortable, and inviting spaces where the users feel comfortable pampering themselves. The bathroom is often the first room entered into in the morning and the last visited before sleep, so it must fully meet the aesthetic and tactile desires of the occupant.

Guest bathrooms present a special design environment due to their traditionally small size. Stronger, more vibrant colors can be used safely in this space without being overwhelming. Where a fire engine red living room might induce headaches, this color in a small bathroom would be striking.

Reaching a balance between form and function in the bathroom can be challenging, but if done correctly, will provide an environment that is both durable and inviting.

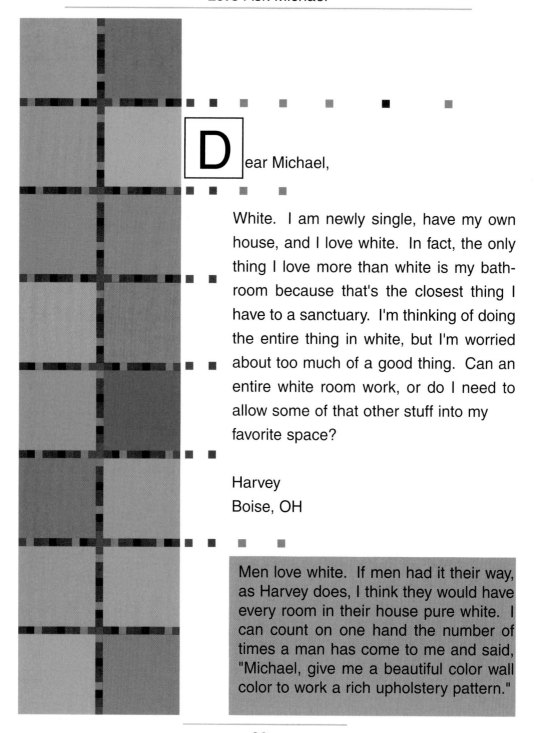

D

ear Michael,

White. I am newly single, have my own house, and I love white. In fact, the only thing I love more than white is my bathroom because that's the closest thing I have to a sanctuary. I'm thinking of doing the entire thing in white, but I'm worried about too much of a good thing. Can an entire white room work, or do I need to allow some of that other stuff into my favorite space?

Harvey
Boise, OH

Men love white. If men had it their way, as Harvey does, I think they would have every room in their house pure white. I can count on one hand the number of times a man has come to me and said, "Michael, give me a beautiful color wall color to work a rich upholstery pattern."

If you love white as much as it sounds like you do, I think the bathroom is the ideal place to do a room entirely in white. The client whose project is pictured below requested exactly that of me. There is white marble tile in the shower and around the tub, and on certain parts of the floor. The remainder of the floor had pure white carpeting. Finding slabs of pure white marble was a challenge as often gray veins are visible. White fixtures are readily available, and there is also a limited selection of purely white faucets. Finally, there are the detail items, such as door hinges and pulls, soap dishes, and bathtub soap dispensers. These you may have to have powder coated, as there is not much demand for them. Add white fluffy towels and a white bathrobe and you're in a white wonderland. All it needs is a magnificently colored flower or two, or some other colorful item you find exci-t ing. This splash will make all the difference in the world, and help accentuate the otherwise entirely white space.

Photography by Douglas Stone

Dear Michael,

I love my wife, but she's driving me nuts about the most inane of things -- our bathtub. She keeps covering it in flowers, squeeze toys, dolls, and even framed pictures! Not only is this far too feminine, it's impractical. Can you suggest a way of decorating the tub while avoiding these pitfalls?

Trent
Worcester, MA

The answer is directly related to how the tub is used. It sounds as though your wife is more concerned with its appearance than its function, so I advise you keep around the tub those items that not only look lovely but will enhance its use. I would include candles, bath oils, and soaps, as these are pleasing to both the eye and the bath user. Framed pictures are definitely not advised as they could easily get destroyed by a soaking, or the dampness that results from the tub. The humidity and natural light can encourage plants to flourish and they add the soft touch of nature to a bath which is, in itself, a treat. By all means make it romantic and inviting, but also keep it functional.

Dear Michael,

My husband and I are sick of having a long counter-top in our bathroom. We think it looks like one found in a cheap hotel's bathroom, and want to go upscale a bit. Any tips?

Sherri and Patrick
Palm Springs, CA

Long vanities in a bathroom can be uninteresting, but are considered advantageous because of the storage they afford. Since you did not reference storage, separate pedestal sinks are one answer. As you can see in the photograph, with a small cabinet between, there is sufficient counter space to keep a smattering of items. With a different layout of the bathroom, two separate vanities can be used instead of a long single one. This allows them to be of different heights and widths to accommodate your individual needs.

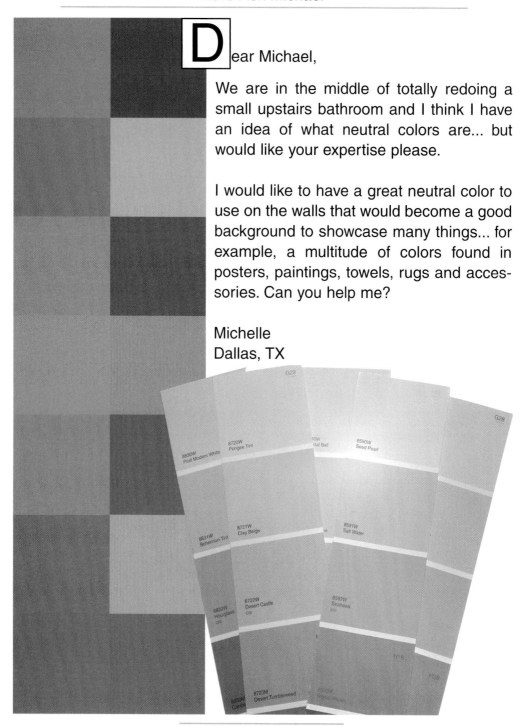

D|ear Michael,

We are in the middle of totally redoing a small upstairs bathroom and I think I have an idea of what neutral colors are... but would like your expertise please.

I would like to have a great neutral color to use on the walls that would become a good background to showcase many things... for example, a multitude of colors found in posters, paintings, towels, rugs and accessories. Can you help me?

Michelle
Dallas, TX

A bathroom in a neutral color. Below, sage green will work with almost anything.

Neutral colors are those that do not compete with other colors. The most often-used neutrals are beiges. Blues, greens, browns, and whites look particularly nice against beiges. Light grey is also considered a neutral color because almost all colors work well with it (however, it tends to be a cold color). Sage green is called "the new neutral" because many colors and woods look wonderful against it.

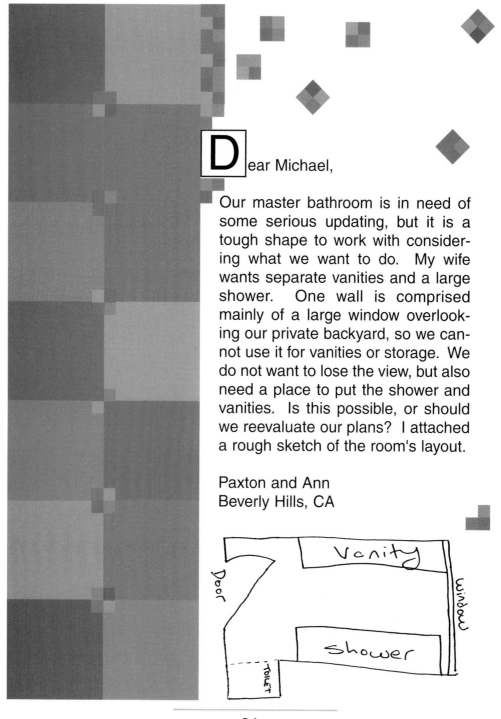

D ear Michael,

Our master bathroom is in need of some serious updating, but it is a tough shape to work with considering what we want to do. My wife wants separate vanities and a large shower. One wall is comprised mainly of a large window overlooking our private backyard, so we cannot use it for vanities or storage. We do not want to lose the view, but also need a place to put the shower and vanities. Is this possible, or should we reevaluate our plans? I attached a rough sketch of the room's layout.

Paxton and Ann
Beverly Hills, CA

You should consider a large double shower with a frameless shower enclosure, two shower heads oriented toward your private exterior view. I suggest you tile your walls and floors in limestone tiles, using smaller size tiles on the shower floor and larger tiles on the walls. The larger limestone tiles, in the photo below, are carried throughout the rest of the bathroom using a diagonal pattern for contrast and interest.

I like the idea of separate vanities. For dramatic contrast to the limestone, have the vanities made with rich brown marble counters and deep stained cabinetry. If you place the vanities on opposite sides of the bathroom, they can even be different heights. In the bathroom shown here, the taller husband had his vanity at 38 inches high and the shorter wife had her vanity at 34 inches high.

ear Michael,

Your show should come with a disclaimer that reads, "Warning: Watching *Designing for the Sexes* will induce the urge to splurge." Every time I watch your show, I want to run out and buy a new snazzy bit of what-have-you for my house. Naturally, I can't afford to do that every week, so I have a question for you. What should I do with my bathroom sink cabinet to make it more interesting? I can't afford to get a new one, but this generic wood one just isn't doing it for me.

Ali
Portland, OR

The best and most effective way to breath new life into a stale piece of furniture if you are on a tight

budget is to have it professionally painted. With the help of the right painter, you can give it nearly any look you can think of. You can have your pick of a cherry, redwood, maple, or oak cabinet that looks either new or worn. The sink at right, for example, looks old but is actually newly painted to look aged.

D ear Michael,

This is a real shot in the dark, but have you ever heard of someone with a relatively small bathroom wanting a separate shower and bathtub, along with separate vanities and, of course, a toilet? Think it's possible?

Riley
New York, NY

I have indeed heard of people wanting this, and I have designed bathrooms with this exact request in mind. The key to successfully executing it is to waste as little space as possible. Try to minimize the space between the individual elements, and be willing to sacrifice some storage space in the interest of fitting everything in. One effective method I have used is to put the bathtub, shower, and toilet on the same wall, with the latter hidden behind the shower's wall. Your vanities will not be expansive, but you can definitely find two that will fit both your space and your needs.

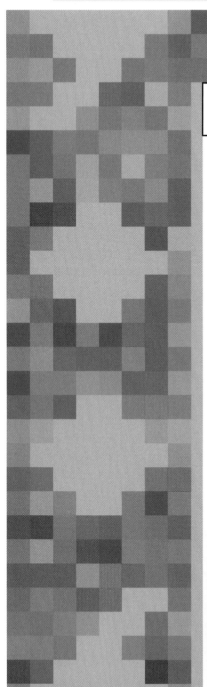

D ear Michael,

I do not pretend to be an expert on Japanese culture or design, but I know I enjoy being in Japanese restaurants and similarly decorated spaces. I am hoping to bring this inside my house via my master bedroom and bathroom. I am nearly done with the bedroom, but am stuck on my bathroom. I do not know how to make a practical American bathroom in the Japanese style, especially given that every bathtub I find would never work in a Japanese space. I included a picture of my house's exterior.

Warren and Linda
Los Angeles, CA

Wood soaking tubs are very popular in Japan, so you might want to consider a wooden hot tub for your bathroom. These tubs are tall, so you will need to provide steps to comfortably enter and exit the tub. It is customary to wash your feet before entering the bathtub, so you should provide a washing place nearby. This will require a drain in the floor, so make sure you can slope the floor appropriately before undertaking the project.

Sliding wood shutters and shoji doors will add to the Japanese ambiance. Keep the whole design simple and minimal with a noted absence of ornamentation and decorative items.

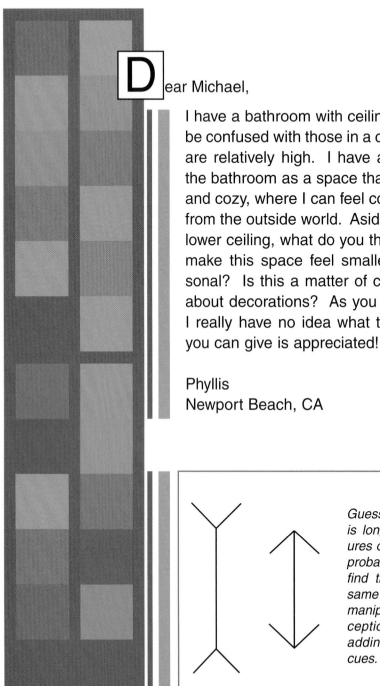

D ear Michael,

I have a bathroom with ceilings that would not be confused with those in a cathedral, but they are relatively high. I have always thought of the bathroom as a space that should be small and cozy, where I can feel completely isolated from the outside world. Aside from installing a lower ceiling, what do you think I should do to make this space feel smaller and more personal? Is this a matter of color, or is it more about decorations? As you can probably tell, I really have no idea what to do so any help you can give is appreciated!

Phyllis
Newport Beach, CA

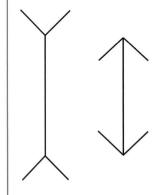

Guess which vertical line is longer in the two figures on the left. You will probably be surprised to find they are the exact same length. One can manipulate people's perceptions of height by adding simple visual cues.

The Bathroom

The crown moulding gives the walls a place to stop.

Well-defined trim around windows defines the normal height of windows.

A darker ceiling color makes it appear lower.

Stone tile on the floor has a heavy look and "anchors" the room.

Photography by Santiago Irigoyen

The tile below the chair rail adds visual weight to the lower half of the room

Running tile to the ceiling defines the shower

Frameless shower doors give the room spacious, airy feel.

Art breaks up the vertical spaces.

Dark tile line at floor level adds more visual weight to bottom of the room.

Decorative tile line at chair rail height vertically divides the room in half.

Photography by Santiago Irigoyen

ear Michael,

I find most medicine cabinets quite ugly and space inefficient. What do you do when you want to install one in a
small bathroom so that it won't intrude too much into the
limited counter space?

Nicole and Steve
Jacksonville, FL

I must admit there are almost no purchasable medicine
cabinets I like. I have a cabinet manufacturer make me a
box with glass adjustable shelves that fits into the wall so
that it is nearly flush with the drywall. The thicker the wall,
the deeper the box can be. Using Blum adjustable hinges,
a mirrored door can be attached to the box and it will lay
flat on the box frame and drywall. It will appear to be just
a wood frame mirror hanging on the wall and not a medicine cabinet at all. The mirror's frame can be as ornate or
simple as you desire.

Pictured below is an example of such a medicine cabinet.
There is no hint the closed mirror conceals a wealth of personal items. The effect is both aes-
thetically pleasing and functionally
successful.

D ear Michael,

I am redoing my son's bathroom and would like to make it really special for him, completely different from all of his friends. Obviously different can be a very bad thing, so do you have any tips for distinctive-yet-tasteful?

Mari
Washington, DC

It really depends on what your son enjoys, be it fire trucks, cars, animals, comics, or anything else. Whatever it is, decorate the bathroom entirely around that theme. My son was particularly passionate about fish as a child, and I created an under water environment by using a wall paper type graphic which was wonderfully playful featuring rabbit-fish, duck-fish, cat-fish, and the

like. As the art's primary background color was deep green, that same tone was used for all cabinetry, trim, and the ceiling. An aquarium completed the theme. Entering that bathroom was like entering another world -- an underwater fantasy land... and my son loved it!

Photography by Andrew Strauss

D ear Michael,

I have always thought stone and mosaic are absolutely beautiful ways of covering surfaces in any room. I have been looking for a place to really let this preference run wild, but am worried a room done in all stone will feel like a cave. Would it be better to do a large or a small room? Do you have any suggestions for which room I should try this in? Have you ever done a room that is essentially all stone? Do you think I've asked you enough questions yet?!

Brian
San Diego, CA

I once designed a guest powder room that did not have one square corner in it. Every plane and each intersection was curved, including the ceiling. Making the project even more difficult was the fact that much of the room was covered with tiles, which are made curved at tremendous expense. The tile layer wanted to kill me during the project because he had to cut out countless tiles to follow the curves. Afterwards he said, "Michael, if I just made my Sistine Chapel, it better be in history books while I'm alive."

There are very few materials in a home that are as impressive as natural stone. It is a huge and varied field encompassing marble, granite, limestone, slate, travertine, and so forth. The stone comes in various colors, thicknesses, finishes, shapes and sizes, porosity, and hardness. Stone is wonderful on floors because it is practical and will last a lifetime. Some people think it is visually cold, so I often use area rugs to soften the space and to add color.

If you are thinking of using the stone on the walls, I recommend doing this in a relatively small space, such as a bathroom. It is typical, of course, to cover the walls of a shower in stone, but I would be hesitant to do every wall in a whole room. It will, as you put it, "feel like a cave." In small rooms, like a guest powder room, you can have the time of your life with various shapes and sizes of stone tile and mosaics. Because of the small size of such a room, hopefully the costs will not be prohibitive. As a final note, using stone in the entrance to your home can make a grand statement.

ear Michael,

I've been wanting to paint my bathroom sink for a while now after seeing it in a New York hotel. Now that I've finally got around to getting it done, I don't have a clue how to paint it! The hotel I was in had it painted with a red and orange pattern that matched the walls, but my walls are just a shade of beige. I know I haven't given you much to work with, but any help would be great.

Paula
Amarillo, TX

You have to consider two factors when painting your sink -- color and design. The color should be inspired by a dominant design detail so that clearly incorporates the room's design. You do not neces-sarily have to copy the wall color, but make sure the two do not clash. The design of the painting should be in keeping with the overall style of the room. Look to tile patterns, rug designs, and paint detailing for inspiration. The other option is to make a bold statement in the painting that does not directly bor-row from anything else in the room, but rather serves as a surprising facet that is as exciting as it is sur-prising. The sink pictured borrows its color and design from the bathroom's tile border.

Dear Michael,

I was thinking about putting some storage and display cabinets in my kid's bathroom, but then thought the moisture from the shower might make this a bad idea. Do you ever have people display their collections in the bathroom, or should we try to put it out in the living room?

Dee
Chattanooga, TN

Bathrooms can display collectibles and personal accessories as well as any other room in your house, provided you have sufficient space. Often people are concerned with how to fit the necessary appliances into one room, let alone leave display

space. If you do have space, then feel free to build any form of cabinetry you desire. The only danger of displaying personal items in a bathroom is they could be damaged by airborne moisture. In this case, install rubber insulating material to diminish the airflow between the cabinets and the room.

chapter 3

the living room

Take one spacious room, add a fireplace, a few comfortable couches, a chair or two, and an ottoman and you are on your way to having a living room. This is the entertainment room that does not have a surround sound system, but is instead used to chat with guests over dinner or drinks. They are typically more formal than family rooms, but have the same emphasis put on comfort. After all, you would not want your guests to leave your house with sore backs from uncomfortable seating.

Formality takes all different shapes and sizes. Some opt for classic Victorian-era design that would not feel out of place in an eighteenth century British castle, while others favor the modern feeling popular in new high-end hotels. Regardless of your taste, make sure you do not concentrate too much on the room's styling and forget that it is still in your house. Decorate the space however you see fit while being mindful that each piece works with the next.

Dear Michael

I have a traditional style fireplace in my living room with a brick surround and white mantel. The existing wide paneled walls are also painted white. The fireplace seems to fade into the wall. How can I create more drama and visual interest to make the fireplace and wall more special? I want to save as much money as possible, so I would like to avoid changing the materials of the fireplace.

Kathy
Austin TX

Consider painting the existing white paneled walls a rich dark color, such as aubergine (eggplant). In a high gloss finish, this color will contrast nicely with the white mantel and really make it pop out visually as well as add dimension to the space. Accessorize your mantel with a grouping of decorative accessories to create a special focal point. Be sure not to clutter the mantel.

D

ear Michael,

We just moved into a brand new, big white contemporary house. We wouldn't have bought it if we didn't love it, but it has become such a challenge. Some of the rooms, the living room for example, have really high ceilings -- probably around 20 feet. We have a lot of furniture from our old house, but it looks completely dwarfed. We are happy buying new furniture, but aside from visiting an NBA player's estate sale, don't think anything will be big enough. Any advice?

Connor and Gwen
Portland, OR

Think big and heavy. Consider dark floors, such as walnut stained wood or dark stone, to anchor the floor. They can always be softened with area rugs. The upholstered furniture should be large in scale, and use darker fabrics to give the pieces weight. Hang large paintings, tapestries, or a large mirror on the walls to break up the space. If you have good light, you might even consider a tall tree. Finally, an over-scaled fireplace, like the one at right, adds scale to the enormous room.

D ear Michael,

We just recently bought a house and the living room has a large brick fireplace on one wall. We don't mind a little brick, but the wall to wall, floor to ceiling brick is overwhelming. We would like to tone it down. Is this possible?

Bernard
Denver, CO

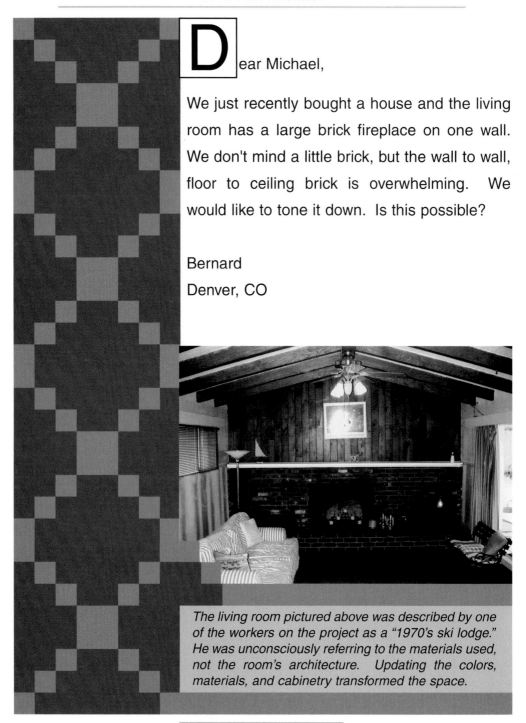

The living room pictured above was described by one of the workers on the project as a "1970's ski lodge." He was unconsciously referring to the materials used, not the room's architecture. Updating the colors, materials, and cabinetry transformed the space.

I suggest you install a painted wood mantel around the firebox, leaving sufficient brick around the firebox to provide the noncombustible area required by code. Apply stucco over the brick above the mantel, creating a wall that you can paint to match the other walls in your living room. Consider covering the brick on either side of the firebox with cabinetry and use it for storage and the display of decorative accessories. You will end up with an attractive focal wall in your living room instead of a wall of red brick. The photograph (*below*) of one of my projects shows the look you can achieve by covering all the brick except that in the firebox.

Dear Michael,

My wife and I have lived in our 1972 house for the past four years, and have been redoing it room by room. We are stuck in our living room, and hope you can give us some advice.

There are holes cut in the wall that allow us to look into the dining room, but we don't like this look. The trouble is we don't know what to do about it. It seems like a lot of work to redo the entire wall just to rid ourselves of these holes, but we don't know what else to do!

Calvin and Brynn
Monroe, WI

I have seen many homes where there have been dividing walls between rooms with openings cut into the walls for decorative purposes. One show had such a room. I closed the opening to the dining room with drywall so in the dining room we now have a solid wall for the display of art. On the living room side, I cased out the opening and

added a sill and shelving for depth. Lighting can be added to the niches and the resulting effect is beautiful areas for the display of favorite collectibles. The inside of these niches can be painted a different color than the rest of the room for an even more dramatic effect.

Dear Michael,

Please help us! Our living room is so boring. We just moved into our very first home and everything is neutral... the floor tiles, the walls and even our brand new cream colored sofas (recently purchased before the move). We do not want to replace the sofas, but we are desperate to interject some color into this very important space. Please help us overcome our paralysis!

Pete and Sheri
St. Louis, MO

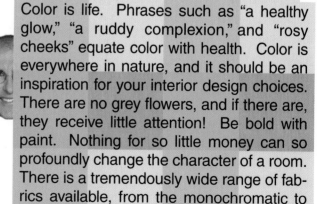

Color is life. Phrases such as "a healthy glow," "a ruddy complexion," and "rosy cheeks" equate color with health. Color is everywhere in nature, and it should be an inspiration for your interior design choices. There are no grey flowers, and if there are, they receive little attention! Be bold with paint. Nothing for so little money can so profoundly change the character of a room. There is a tremendously wide range of fabrics available, from the monochromatic to those that look like a rainbow in a blender!

Don't be paralyzed! You have a lot of options to consider without changing your sofas. These photos of one of my projects show the transformation you can expect. Adding color and accessories to your living room will do wonders to warm this space and make it more attractive.

Consider using one wall as an accent wall by painting it a different color

than the rest of your walls. If you have a fireplace, use the fireplace wall as your accent wall. Keep the trim in the room white to add contrast and crispness. Add an area rug and decorative throw pillows for more color and texture. Place special decorative items on a coffee table as well as on your fireplace mantel. Use decorative table lamps and/or floor lamps for accent lighting.

Dear Michael,

We have a great piece of art that we want to be the center of attention in our living room, but the trouble is that it simply isn't very big. I have always heard that the space above the fireplace is a good place to hang art, but I think this painting will be totally lost up there. We want it to be impactful, not look like a speck on the wall! Do you have any tips?

Carlos and Mary
Poughkeepsie, NY

A fireplace with faux inlayed framing.

I actually had a nearly identical circumstance in one of my projects, so you can take heart in the fact that your problem is not unique, nor is it difficult to solve. I had an artist paint a faux recess on the fireplace wall which continues to trick even myself into thinking I ordered an expensive structural change of the wall. Having measured the clients' art which was to hang there, I had the artist paint the "recess" to the ideal size for the painting. The shadows of the recess were exactly where they would

have been had it been real. The finished product fooled everyone who saw it, and the previously dwarfed painting looked perfect in the space.

True faux painting, like the example pictured on these pages, can be incredibly effective. Niches can be created with vases and flowers standing inside, windows can be created with magnificent views, and insects can even be painted onto the wall. It can be particularly effective in a child's room, where an entire environment can be created. When the budget does not allow for the real thing, faux painting can offer nearly the same effect at the fraction of the cost.

Dear Michael,

In your shows it's all about color. But what do you do with people like us who do not like strong colors? We want an interesting room that is not overflowing with flowery colors and crazy patterns.

Patrick and Deanne

Watertown, CT

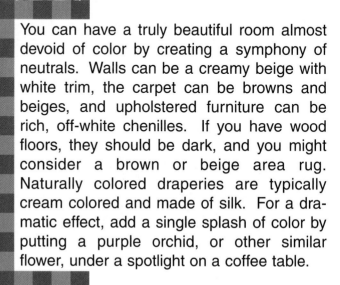

You can have a truly beautiful room almost devoid of color by creating a symphony of neutrals. Walls can be a creamy beige with white trim, the carpet can be browns and beiges, and upholstered furniture can be rich, off-white chenilles. If you have wood floors, they should be dark, and you might consider a brown or beige area rug. Naturally colored draperies are typically cream colored and made of silk. For a dramatic effect, add a single splash of color by putting a purple orchid, or other similar flower, under a spotlight on a coffee table.

II always give my clients what they want, and I never force color on any-one. One can create beautiful neutral environments using various shades of grays and beiges. Black can make a strong statement when used judiciously. I believe there should be some color and it can be added in spaces by using art or decorative accessories like pillows.

In this particular room, the largest furniture items are upholstered in

shades of brown and gray. The walls are a neutral beige color, and even items like the lamp, dresser, and fire-place screen are primarily black and white. Small splashes of color from the rose throw pillow, yellow vase, and antique poster add life to this room while not saturating it with color.

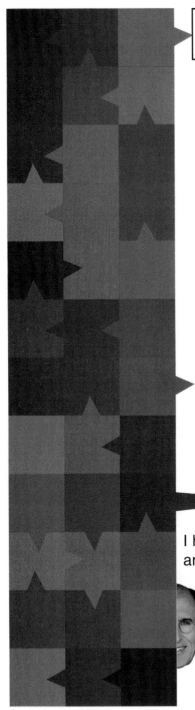

Dear Michael,

I have a huge brick fireplace in a corner of my living room. I don't know if the people who built my house owned a brick factory or something, but this fireplace is absolutely enormous. It dominates the entire room, and it doesn't even have a mantel!

Can you suggest any way to make this eye sore a bit more sightly, without having to remove the whole thing?

Ronald and Lea

Boston, MA

I have changed more fireplaces than any other architectural detail. Fireplaces say so much about a room and often new owners do not like what they hear! Covering brick with plaster or stucco is an inexpensive way of eliminating a visual aggravation. The wall can then be painted, or a mantel installed, and these changes can completely alter the look of the room.

You can soften the look of the fireplace by adding a full mantel around the firebox, or just adding a mantel shelf. This shelf can be either painted or stained, according to what complements your room and works with the brick's tone. By adding your favorite decorative accessories to the mantel, you should be able to finally tame your big brick fireplace!

Putting a mantel on an oversized fireplace serves a dual purpose. The first is that it visually splits the space, making it not feel so enormous. Second, it gives a fantastic opportunity to add some visual excitement beyond the repeating brick pattern, or if the fireplace is painted, beyond the large monotone color. In the fireplace pictured on the right, the owner used the mantel to showcase his love of the nautical world. The boat illustration and model both add a personal touch, while making the space more interesting.

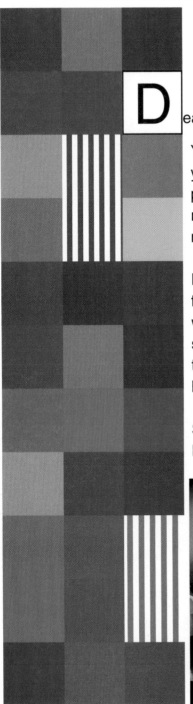

Dear Michael,

You know how you never really know what you're missing until you see what other people have? Well, thanks to your show I've realized my living room is Boring (please note the capital "B").

It's a long, narrow room with a fireplace flanked by two windows, and a sofa on the wall opposite the fireplace. Since the room is so narrow, I don't think I can do any of the things I've seen on TV. Am I stuck with this boring room?

Sheila
Hastings, NE

I'm sorry to say that if your room is narrow, placing the sofa across from the fireplace is the only thing you can do. Putting it perpendicular will effectively create a roadblock. However, with side tables next to the sofa and two lounge chairs, you can have a very nice seating group all centered around the fireplace.

Now let's address the boring look you mention. When you are choosing the coffee table, consider something a little different from the standard items you'll find in a local, mass production store. You could use a chest, an ottoman, or even a small wagon with a glass on top. Anchor this seating group with an area rug that brings color and exciting detail to the room. Pull out a color from the rug for the walls or the fabrics you are using.

Finally, it is important to accessorize the room to relieve the tedium. Display your favorite collectibles in key locations, but be careful not to clutter. Once you've taken these steps, your room will be anything but Boring.

Dear Michael,

My wife and I are planning on redoing our living room, but we are at a stylistic impasse. I am very fond of the newest trends in design which feature steel, brushed aluminum, and various light metals. My wife moved to America from Japan a number of years ago and would like to incorporate some traditional elements from her culture into the living room. I know mixing these two is possible because I saw an episode of your show where you did something like this. Would you mind briefly discussing some important elements of this design so that my wife and I could try to do it ourselves?

Bo and Yaeka
Beverly Hills, CA

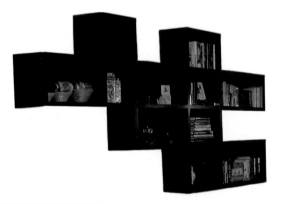

You will be pleased to hear you and your wife's tastes are not terribly dis-similar, as they both start with simplicity. In the project you referenced, the client had an extensive collection of oversized books and Asian arti-facts. I needed a way to display them while keeping an uncluttered look to the room. The bookcase design incorporated individual compartments for display by using defined horizontal and vertical lines. Likewise, the furniture had the same simple, unadorned vertical lines. There was no ornamentation whatsoever. The drapes were a simple piece of solid fab-ric suspended on a stainless steel rod that could be lowered to cover the window. The simple, geometric theme was further carried on by the area rug, which was a series of squares in various shades of gray. Finally, the basic theme of the room were colors chosen so that everything was neu-tral. Stronger color was introduced from the art and books, and red, by design, was the punch. To subtly enhance this Asian sensibility, a silver metallic shaft of light was painted on the wall from the ceiling skylight to, and around, the fireplace.

D ear Michael,

I have a living room that has a rock fireplace which is so country I feel as though I should have cows in my backyard! Making it even more out of place is the fact that I live in a big city, so I want a cosmopolitan look. My budget is tight, and I can't afford to re-do the fireplace. How can I get a more sophisticated look? Thank you for your help!

Asher

San Diego, CA

For the moment, forget the fireplace and concentrate on the furnishings in the room. Stay away from cold steel and glass, and introduce the warmth of woods in contemporarily styled tables. These will have straight, tapered legs, and will have little or no ornamentation. Sofas and chairs can be angular, but should not have rolled arms. These add a traditional feeling that you seem to want to avoid. Fabrics should be plain or geometric. By outfitting your room like this, the fireplace will actually not need to be touched and will make for an interesting stylistic juxtaposition. While fireplaces are dominant elements in a room, their impact can be offset by correctly styling the rest of the room.

Dear Michael,

Our living room looks like a high school gymnasium with it's great length and polished wood floors. My husband and I feel like most of it is wasted space and we don't know what to do with it. For one thing, it feels more like a warehouse than it does a living room, and for another we have basically no use for anything in it. We have been reluctant to buy furniture for fear of its getting lost in the space, but need something so we can entertain guests. How can we fill the space without buying 20 foot long sofas?

Percy and Alissa
Athens, GA

Attempting to furnish a long, narrow room with a single seating arrangement can be a daunting task. Even if you do succeed, you risk ending up with something that looks like a business conference room instead of a warm, inviting, living room. The approach I much prefer in furnishing such spaces is to divide the room into more manageable sizes. In photograph 3 below, the entry into the long space is close to the middle of the room, naturally dividing the room in half. I needed to relocate a piano (*see opposite page*), and in doing so created two distinctly separate seating groups, pictured in 1 and 2 below. Area rugs and different but complementary fabrics define each group. Not only does the room function better with more open and accessible spaces, but there is no wasted space.

Dear Michael,

I'm a pack rat, and I have acquired an incredible collection of framed items. I hesitate to say it's all art because some of it is work my kids did, other pieces are movie posters, and then there is the 'real' art collection. I definitely have too much to hang, but I'm constrained by the "one piece per wall" rule my friends insist is the gospel. Is this an absolute rule, or can you suggest a way to hang multiple pieces on one wall?

Katy and Johnson
Bellevue, WA

While there will always be differing opinions about what is good and bad design, one of the reasons there is such diversity in interior design is because there are no set rules. In every culture there is an expression that essentially says, "beauty is in the eye of the beholder." You should feel free to arrange your collection of pieces in a way you feel is pleasing to the eye, and reflective of the artistry within the works. I prefer a sense of order, so I tend to arrange multiple items on a wall with edges lining up horizontally and vertically, but this is not the only way.

In the photographs (*left and above*), you see several large pieces arranged as though they are in a gallery or a museum. There are several pieces on the same segment of wall but it does not look overdone or cluttered. Let your eye be the judge, and if you think what you are doing looks good, break any rules your friends impose on you.

Dear Michael,

This is just a general question about living rooms. We have a room that is the product of 8 years of randomly adding things -- couches, chairs, an entertainment cabinet, and a few other items. None of them fit well together, and we're wondering what you always include in those fancy living rooms we've seen on your show. Any tips you can give would be great. Thanks!

Joshua and Lilly
Pocatello, ID

The first thing you need to decide is what style you want for the room. Once this is decided, evaluate every piece of existing furniture in the room and judge its appropriateness. I am sorry to say it is probable that several pieces will have to find a home in other rooms or in someone else's home. The benefit

of removing some of these pieces is that you will be free to furnish and decorate without the constraints of past decisions. With new fabrics, new furniture, color on the walls, and decorative accessories, your living room will be just as special as anything you have seen on television.

chapter 4

the kitchen

The kitchen is dedicated to a single purpose that is unfortunately not a clean one. Regardless of whether you are an internationally renowned chef or a novice spaghetti creator, the food you enjoy is not the only thing cooking creates. Oils are spilled, noodles are dropped, flour is strewn, and eggs are splattered. All of this would be less problematic if kitchens were made of a single pieces of stainless steel, but people like warmth in the kitchen.

The challenge is to not compromise the functionality of your kitchen while keeping it from feeling like an operating room. There is a wide breadth of materials that are both pleasing to the eye and resilient to damage. The details of a kitchen, such as the cabinet pulls, tile design, and countertop accessories, are the owner's place to instill personality into this utilitarian space.

D ear Michael,

I always love rooms that have a lot of stone work in them... they look so sturdy, so stalwart, and so sensible. I'm redoing my kitchen, and I don't want to be afraid to spill some soup or drop an egg for fear of ruining the space. How do you suggest, Michael, I work a heavy stone theme into my new kitchen?

Madeline
Brentwood, CA

The Kitchen

You are fortunate to love a material that is both practical and beautiful, and your kitchen is the perfect place to enjoy all of its virtues. There are at least four places where stone can be used. The first is counters, which would ideally be sealed marble or granite, but could also be a sealed limestone or soapstone. The second place is the backsplash, which can either be the same as the counter's material, or a contrasting material. Third, if you have a hood, you can consider covering it with stone, and it can pick up the colors of the splash, colors of the wall, or something completely different. Finally, the floor can be finished in any of a multitude of stone sizes and variations. Slate is particularly practical because it does not show dirt, is non-skid, and comes in a wide range of neutral colors. If you have a breakfast nook, consider something unique like a marble mosaic top.

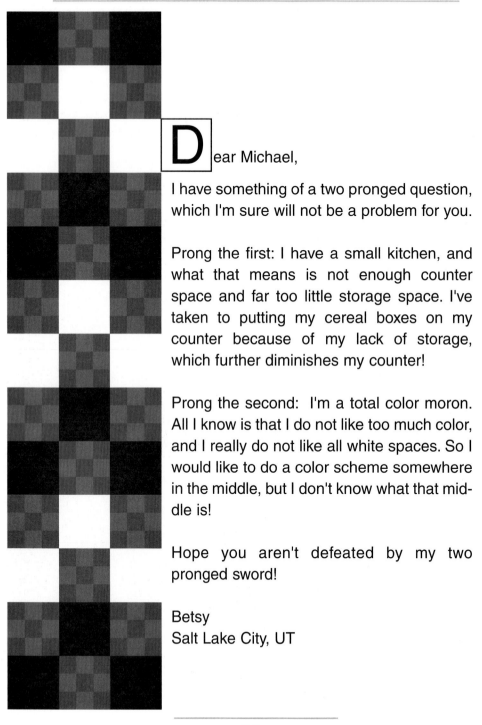

D ear Michael,

I have something of a two pronged question, which I'm sure will not be a problem for you.

Prong the first: I have a small kitchen, and what that means is not enough counter space and far too little storage space. I've taken to putting my cereal boxes on my counter because of my lack of storage, which further diminishes my counter!

Prong the second: I'm a total color moron. All I know is that I do not like too much color, and I really do not like all white spaces. So I would like to do a color scheme somewhere in the middle, but I don't know what that middle is!

Hope you aren't defeated by my two pronged sword!

Betsy
Salt Lake City, UT

When you have a small kitchen it is imperative you utilize every inch of the space. First, the upper cabinets should go to the ceiling, which you can access by using a foot stool. The lower cabinets should have pull out shelves to decrease the likelihood that there are forgotten items nestled at the back. Install lazy susans in the corners to further maximize the space (this will turn otherwise unusable areas into functional storage spaces). These rotating shelves can be used for the storage of small-to-medium sized appliances. Keep appliances off the counters if at all possible.

The placement of a microwave oven is often problematic due to the frequency with which they are used and their relatively large size. In lower cabinets they are too low and in upper cabinets they are too high. If there is space on either side of the splash, recess the microwave into the wall.

Kitchens can be a kaleidoscope of color or monochromatic. I suggest you consider either stained wood cabinets or cabinets painted in a very light neutral color. Both this color and wood allow you to choose a variety of materials for the counters and backsplash. These, too, can be neutral but would ideally add some contrast and visual life. Lastly, choose a paint color for your walls that is somewhat bold. Typically there is not a lot of wall space in kitchens, so this allows for an exciting paint color.

Photography by Christopher Covey

Dear Michael,

You're going to roll your eyes when I tell you my problem. I don't like monotone tile treatments, and I don't like patterns. In other words, I don't like one color kitchen counters, and I don't like cute tile patterns with lots of neat colors. My husband, predictably, does not share my taste. He wants a nice, traditional kitchen his mother will be proud of. What do you think?

Samantha
Los Angeles, CA

Assuming you want to stay with tile, there are many ways to use tile in an unconventional, unpredictable, yet tasteful manner. There is an entire world of decorative tile, so you will no doubt be able to find a set that excites you. You can find tiles with nearly anything you can imagine, including birds, flowers, fruits, vegetables, cars, houses, and fashion items. Once you find a set of tiles that pleases you, you can arrange them randomly around the kitchen, adding a delightfully surprising facet to your kitchen's interior. To satisfy your husband's need for tradition, consider running a decorative tile border along the edge of your counters.

I placed vegetable and wine tiles around the kitchen pictured to create a fresh, country feel that reflected the client's love of wine.

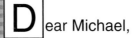

D ear Michael,

You're creative and we're not, and that's why we are emailing you. We have a kitchen that makes a campsite look luxurious, and we are hoping you will give us as many ideas as you can for ways to make a kitchen exciting, personal, and individual. We probably won't be able to use every idea you give, but any inspiration will be of use to this creatively challenged couple! We look forward to hearing from you.

Mike and Lucinda
Newark, NJ

These before shots depict a kitchen that desperately needed a redesign. It was completely devoid of personally defined elements and any inspired design and decoration.

Photography by Christopher Covey

This kitchen is rife with unique and personal details. The custom backsplash (left) depicts the family's pets, the teapots reflect their interest in animals and English heritage, and the display space allows for tremendous versatility in decorating. Great care was taken to ensure the counters (green granite), back splash (slate), cabinets (stained maple), floor (ceramic tile), and wall color (beige) worked beautifully together. The result is a stunning, yet functional, workplace.

Photography by Christopher Covey

Dear Michael,

My wife and I don't have much of a wine collection, but we can't figure out a convenient place to keep a dozen or so bottles on hand. Do you have any suggestions?

Ferdinand and Julia
Shreveport, LA

To cool or not to cool, that is the question. Wine refrigerators come 24" wide and fit under the counter like a dish washer. Otherwise, you can have a handsome storage cabinet in any size that matches the rest of the cabinetry. It is up to you to decide if you like your wine chilled.

D ear Michael,

I couldn't help but notice that the hood in my kitchen takes up a lot of space for pretty much no reason. All it is is a big collector with fans that connects to a pipe, and the rest of it is just empty. I'd like to store a few random items in there, but if I put doors on, they will hit the ceiling when opened. Have you ever heard of a way to make using the hood as storage work successfully?

Jon
Bloomington, IN

I am impressed you even thought to use your hood for storage because many people never consider it as a viable storage space. You can turn it into a cabinet to keep small items by hinging it at the top, and having the forward facing plane swing upward. The hinges will be attached to either a spring or a pneumatic canister so that it will remain open.

Because of the height, this space will probably not be practical for items used daily, but is ideal for those items you only use occasionally. The example below is designed to look like traditionally hinged cabinets for consistency throughout the kitchen, but is actually top-hinged.

Dear Michael,

My wife and I are in the process of redoing our kitchen, and I want to go a little wild with the overall look. I don't want to do anything non-sensically crazy, like put shag carpeting on the countertops, but I would like something that is both exciting and different from what anyone else has. I am thinking of some interesting tile patterns, but realize that unusual tile patterns could turn out to be incredibly ugly. Do you have any tips for making my kitchen crazy in a sane way?

Chuck
Bethesda, MD

I like the idea of using tile in an imaginative and creative way. All too frequently, people want to use a solid surface such as granite or marble for countertops. Your considering tile opens a wonderful world of color and design that classical solid surface solutions do not.

In the photographs (*left and opposite page*), I used some of the most vibrantly colored tile I could find on the counter's border in order to set the palette for the entire kitchen. Variations of these tiles were used everywhere in the kitchen, except the splash and hood, and infused the room with a life that granite or marble would have difficulty equalling. The terracotta color in the border was reflected in the floor, the lighter shade of yellow was used on the walls, and the blue appears on the concrete island.

My tip for success? Attempt to create a harmonious color scheme regardless of how zany you wish to be. The two are not mutually exclusive.

D

ear Michael,

I have always been fond of steel items, but realize overdoing it can make a room look like a morgue. I found a great steel topped table and want to put it in my kitchen. Do you think this is a viable place for such an item?

Paul
Bridgeport, CT

You are right to be wary of overloading a room with steel products unless you are aiming for a modern, sterile look. Steel pieces used in moderation in a setting of warm colors and materials create a dramatic contrast that is both eye catching and functional. The trouble is that the steel will scratch and show finger prints. It is, however, easily cleaned and offers a refreshingly contemporary alternative to wood or glass.

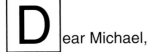ear Michael,

I have noticed in several of my friends' kitchens that they have a tile border on their kitchen floors. I am redoing my kitchen on a tight budget, and would like to know if the final product will be attractive without the outline.

Percy and Emily
Dodge City, KS

Bordering a tile floor has a certain aesthetic appeal, but it is by no means necessary for a successful design. The argument for the border is to clearly define the space, like using an area rug in a room. The argument against it is that without the border, the tile appears to flow unconstrained under the cabinets and appliances, resulting in appearance of a larger space. This is important in smaller kitchens. Running the tile on the diagonal further enhances the sense of space and is visually more stimulating.

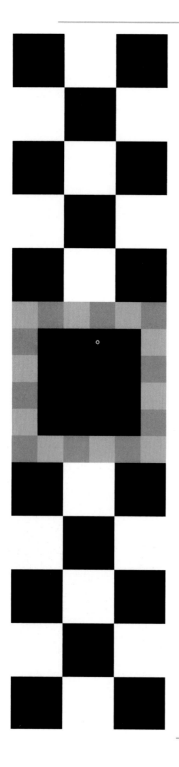

Dear Michael,

I will make no bones about the fact I am an individualist, and I like my material possessions to represent that. My wife does not share this flare for what I call individuality, and which she calls idiocrasy.

We are redoing our kitchen, and while she has the final say on it, I would like to use some materials that are distinctive. What is a wood not often used, and maybe some color combinations not typically seen?

Sal
Aspen, CO

The most interesting rooms will always be the ones where you inject your unique personality. We all know that no two people are the same, so one's home is an ideal place to celebrate one's unique traits. Indulge your tastes that some might consider bizarre.

There are so many way to take what could be a typical kitchen and make it extraordinary. Instead of painting or staining cabinets, they could be dyed with an amaline dye in brilliant colors, or perhaps painted with a metallic paint -- some of which naturally develop a pattern. Use unique pulls on the cabinets, as they are the jewelry of the kitchen.

Doors could have real metal panels in any metal of your choice. Your counters do not have to be tile or granite, but could be concrete, a metal like stainless steel, a butcher block, or a stone like limestone that will be stained through use.

Flooring can be concrete, custom designed vinyl in extraordinary shapes and colors, bamboo wood, plastic laminate, or anything else that will withstand some abuse.

Consider low voltage cable lights instead of recessed lights.

Photography by Christopher Covey

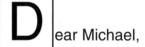

Dear Michael,

Whose idea was it to bring the galley kitchen off the boat? My kitchen is just a long corridor with cabinets, a sink, a stove, etc. lining the walls. It feels so cramped that if not for the view of land out of my window, I would not be surprised if I was indeed on a seagoing vessel. Can you suggest anything to make the space feel larger? Also, on a related note, can you think of a way to provide a small area where several people can eat?

Morgan
St Paul, MN

Bumping out certain areas in a galley kitchen can achieve small miracles. If the window is pushed out and the counter extends into the space, you will achieve an extraordinary feeling of openness in your kitchen (*below*). The additional windows will emit more light and the cramped kitchen will seem to expand into the garden.

A breakfast nook can also successfully be incorporated in the narrow space in exactly the same way. In the photograph (*opposite page*) you will see that with banquette seating, four people can be accommodated in the space the cabinetry used to occupy. There is relatively no infringement on the narrow kitchen's walking space, so all that is lost is some storage space. Notice that the pedestal table takes a minimum of foot-space and has softened corners for ease of use. A galley kitchen will never feel cavernous, but the proper changes will make it feel more like a part of a house than a boat.

D ear Michael,

I'm tired of having my microwave take up valuable counter space. Any suggestions?

You are not alone in your microwave-related space troubles. Many of my clients complain they take up too much space and clutter their counters and shelves. Consider installing it in the upper cabinets, or under the counter (*top*). Both of these suggestions are functionally superior to placing it on the counter, but your microwave will take up other storage space. The best solution is to embed it in the splash (*bottom*), which puts it at counter level without taking any counter space. This solution requires available space behind the splash.

ear Michael,

I find the door pulls in my kitchen to be boring. They're just white plastic semi-circles, and really do nothing for me aesthetically. Can you suggest some other styles?

Pulls are an art form, and I consider them the jewelry of a project. They are made of every conceivable material and are available in countless designs, so you can almost certainly find a pull that excites you. They can make as powerful or subtle a statement as you wish, and their use is only constrained by your willingness to experiment. Contemporary cabinets often have long, simple stainless steel pulls, where traditional cabinets often have round ornamental knobs in antique brass, pewter, or bronze. Country cabinets often draw on natural wood cues and utilize painted or stained wood knobs, or metal knobs that are designed to look worn. Finally, do not forget about specialty knobs, such as animal knobs. You can find pulls in the form of every animal, including the bronze pig I used in my own kitchen.

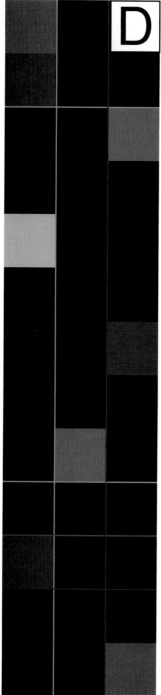

Dear Michael,

Since I watch you on TV every week, I feel like we're friends so I'm going to tell you a brief story. When I was in college, I got in the habit of always working in my kitchen. I don't know why, and my psychology-majoring roommate had a field day with it, but I could always concentrate best in the kitchen. That was almost 20 years ago, and I've converted my guest room into my office, but I still find myself doing a lot of reading in the kitchen. I know I can't move my office into the kitchen, but do you think it's possible to make some space in the kitchen for me to do work?

Perrin
Mobile, AL

The best rule in any design is to fit a space to your needs. Don't be held back by convention or by perceived practicality. Any room can be designed to accommodate your specific needs. A kitchen can be a work area, a gym an office, a bedroom an office, and so on.

You are not alone! A lot of people do work in their kitchens, whether it is preparing recipes, doing homework, or running a business. Ideally, you can set up a dedicated work space at a built-in desk. With a 36" wide desk you can have a bank of drawers on one side that could  include a file drawer. Space allowing, you can install cabinetry above the desk for supplies or shelves for books.

If you do not have sufficient space for a separate desk, the island can make for a work space. In the kitchen below, the client asked for a space where he could use his laptop to do paperwork. We gave him a fairly substantial area for desk space that was far enough from the sink to decrease the likelihood of damaging his work. We put an electrical outlet near the seating area, and the workspace worked out beautifully.

chapter 5

the dining room

There appears to be an inverse relationship between the formality of the dining room and the frequency it is used. The fanciest of dining rooms are largely neglected as places to eat and are favored as three dimensional art pieces, where the less formal ones tend to be used on a more regular basis for their designated dining purpose.

Neither approach is wrong, so it is up to homeowners to determine how the dining room will be used before embarking on remodeling. If it is to be used on a daily basis, it might be advisable to forego expansive on-table ornamentation, delicate antique chairs, and fragile tables in favor of more resilient pieces. Conversely, if the room will not be used often, there are nearly no practical constraints put on the choice of furniture and decoration.

Regardless of whether the dining room is going to be used often or infrequently, it should be decorated such that it is a comfortable place for people to sit over long periods of time. Mixing personal accessories along with serving items will add a personal touch that makes your dining room feel more like a home than a restaurant.

Dear Michael,

I have a dining room/kitchen that is old and has slate and stone everywhere. I have taken to calling it the Bat Cave because that's how dark and cold it feels.

I want to go in the complete opposite direction by making it feel as "country home" as possible. What materials and colors are used for this? Do you have any suggestions?

Bernadette
Jacksonville, FL

Photography by Santiago Irigoyen

Let's talk about what makes country, "country." It's warm, homey and inviting, and it is most certainly the opposite of what you describe as your current dining room and kitchen. A country feeling space is one in which you feel comfortable, secure, relaxed, and hopefully isolated from the city that lies outside your front door. The materials most often used are wood for the cabinets, tile or stone for the counters and backsplash, and either of these materials for the flooring. Stained beams on the ceiling will give the rooms an old world, rustic touch.

Rich colors such as red, terracotta, or gold on the walls will infuse the rooms with an intimate coziness. Fabrics on the dining room chairs and draperies will add to the homey feeling. A lighting fixture over the dining table could be wrought iron and charming, with the rest of the room being lit by low voltage recessed lights and sconces.

D

ear Michael,

My wife and I are in the process of redoing our dining room, and some good friends of ours told us it is important to have a "design motif." First of all, what does that really mean, and secondly, is it particularly important to have in a dining room? Thank you for your input.

Jerry and Liz
South Bend, IN

A design motif is simply a design element or subject that is repeated, often in various guises. I have done rooms where the motif was a particular animal, and I used that theme in art, fabrics, table lamps, rugs, and decorative accessories.

In the photograph at right, the pyramid was the motif. I designed a recess in the ceiling and amplified the motif using cherry detailing with the maple. The cherry cabinets have cherry veneer laid in different directions to create diamonds that echo the theme, the glass in the display doors is etched with the same design, and even the wine rack is consistent with the pyramid motif. All of these elements contribute to an overhaul harmony in the design.

Photography by Christopher Covey

106

Dear Michael,

We had company a few days ago and some of our friends commented that our dining room would not look out of place in the apartment of a kid who just moved away from home. In other words, it looks cheap, and it just flows into the living room. There's no wall separating it from the living room, so there really is just a randomly placed table, some chairs, and nothing else. What do you suggest we do to make this corner of the living room into something that feels more like a dining room (we don't have the budget to install new walls)?

Leonie and Derrick
Temple, AZ

You need to define the dining room space by using distinct visual cues that are separate from the living room. An appropriately sized table that is correctly positioned, whether rectangular or circular, will only start to define the room. An area rug under the table will assist in further defining the space. A pendant light hanging over the table is yet another step, and an accent wall with a buffet table or china cabinet will complete the picture. Stop the accent color

at the corner with as precise a line as you can paint.

In the room pictured, the red wall, imposing table, area rug, and wall decoration work together to create an environment that feels distinctly separate from the adjoining living room (*pictured at left*).

Dear Michael,

We are remodeling our dining room and my husband and I can't agree on a style. The room is 12' x 18', has warm nutmeg wood floors, and is open to the kitchen. The kitchen has the same floors, bisque-colored cabinets and olive, cream, and brown granite countertops. The fireplace in the dining room has floor-to-ceiling bricks and a raised hearth. The bricks have various colors and the fireplace looks very dated. Is there a way to update the fireplace that is not horribly expensive? What about a color scheme, what would look nice with the kitchen colors?

Judy and Lance
Lincoln, NE

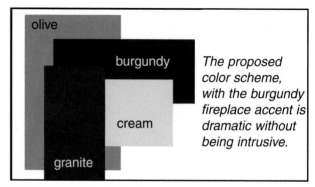

The proposed color scheme, with the burgundy fireplace accent is dramatic without being intrusive.

Regarding the fireplace, you could stucco over the brick and paint it a contrasting color to the walls. The color should relate to the fabric you use on the sofa or on the throw pillows. Because you mentioned having having olive in your kitchen, I would recommend painting the room's walls the same color for continuity. Then you might consider painting the fireplace a contrasting burgundy color, as is pictured below, to create a dramatic accent.

Accent walls, in general, are an economical way of infusing a room with life. They are also an effective way of balancing conservative color preferences with a desire for an interesting, dramatic room. You can get away with a color that would otherwise be rather dull by providing a contrast to it. A beige room will never have the same effect a bright red one will, but adding a bright blue wall to the beige room will certainly point it in the direction of stimulating instead of dull.

Dear Michael,

Good things come in small packages, right? Well we have a tiny (and I mean tiny) dining room that I want to make as elegant and dramatic as possible. The room itself is approximately 10' x 10', with windows on the same wall as the door. So I have 3 walls to deal with that have basically nothing going on.

We don't plan on entertaining large groups of people, so it will just be my husband, my two kids, and I using the room. I am open to any suggestions for how to make a beautiful, exciting room!

Phil and Rhonda,
Rye, NY

There is no reason a small room should not be as dramatic and inviting as a large one. In fact, small rooms provide an intimacy that is hard to achieve in spacious rooms.

As the room is square and there are just the four of you, a square table is the answer. This could have a glass top with an interesting base, perhaps an interesting wrought iron design. This should sit on an area rug that in turn, lays on a hardwood floor. The rug will be clearly visible under the wrought iron and will be seen through the glass.

Choose fabrics that you love for the chairs and draperies, and be careful to ensure their cohesion with the rug. I prefer to use solid drapery fabric instead of translucent, lace ones. Choose a dramatic paint color from the fabrics to use as your wall color.

To make your dining room truly special, consider a shallow wall fountain on one wall and a vent-less gas fireplace for the opposite wall. The sound of the water and the firelight will be extraordinary.

For the room's lighting, a wrought iron chandelier over the table augmented by recessed low voltage adjustable lights to highlight the fountain and fireplace will be the crowning touch.

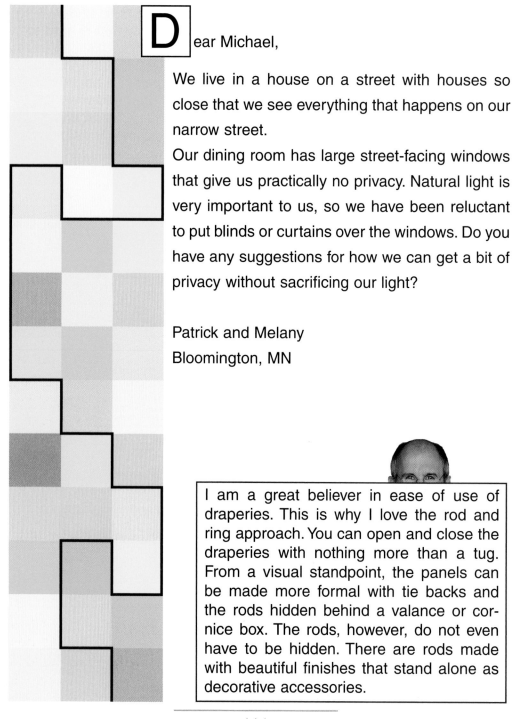

Dear Michael,

We live in a house on a street with houses so close that we see everything that happens on our narrow street.

Our dining room has large street-facing windows that give us practically no privacy. Natural light is very important to us, so we have been reluctant to put blinds or curtains over the windows. Do you have any suggestions for how we can get a bit of privacy without sacrificing our light?

Patrick and Melany
Bloomington, MN

I am a great believer in ease of use of draperies. This is why I love the rod and ring approach. You can open and close the draperies with nothing more than a tug. From a visual standpoint, the panels can be made more formal with tie backs and the rods hidden behind a valance or cornice box. The rods, however, do not even have to be hidden. There are rods made with beautiful finishes that stand alone as decorative accessories.

If you have the double desire of allowing light in through your window while preserving privacy, sheers are the best solution to your problem. You can use a double rod drapery treatment where you have the sheer hanging closest to the window and an over drapery on the outside. The sheers will not only provide you with the natural light you love, but also the privacy you want. The over drapery can stack either side of the window during the day and be closed at night to give you total privacy.

The three pictures at left demonstrate the versatility of the double rod and ring approach. The top photograph supplies maximum privacy with both the sheer and over drapery closed. The middle photograph allows more light in while preserving privacy by stacking the over draperies and keeping the sheer closed. Finally, both the sheer and over drapery are open in the bottom photograph, allowing the view and light to spill into the room.

D

ear Michael,

What do you think about glass tables in the dining room? I know it's traditional to have a large, heavy wood table, but I'm not sure if that fits my taste. Also, I find some wood tables incredibly difficult to clean, with all their little holes and gaps. Sometimes it seems like the table eats more food than the people do, so much food falls into little natural imperfections!

I'm worried for one thing about how a glass table will look in a dining room. Will it look too modern, or too cold? Also, are there special types of glass that prevent scratching, because I'm sure plates, knives, and just general use will mar the finish.

Pam
Lewiston, ME

Glass top dining tables are wonderful alternatives to the classical, traditional wood tops to which people have become accustomed. One benefit of using glass tables is that they have a lighter appearance. This can be significant in smaller spaces, where a solid surface table can appear to consume the space. Another benefit is that area rugs can be seen through the glass top and appreciated to a greater extent. The style of the table will be dictated by the base, which can be literally anything, including wrought iron, wood, stone, concrete, steel, and plastic. It can be tra-

ditional or contemporary depending on your taste.

Glass can easily be kept perfectly clean, but does scratch. If you use decorative items on the table, ensure they have protective pads, and always use place mats or a tablecloth for dining.

Dear Michael,

We have a beige dining room with a recess in the ceiling, and we don't know how to paint it. Do you have any suggestions?

Bentley and Janet
Pawtucket, RI

The recess is an architectural detail that adds interest and visual importance to the dining room. The recess can be painted in a number of different ways, from a solid color to a trompe d'oile scene of clouds with angels. In the dining room pictured on this page, I took a stylistic cue from fabrics on the dining room chairs and stencilled the design around the recess. In addition, I high-lighted parts of the crown moulding to amplify its presence. It was inexpensive to execute and the result was subtle, elegant, and striking.

ear Michael,

I'm in a bit of a bind trying to fill the space in my dining room. I don't have any feeling about what type of items to display, nor do I know how to display them. How do you advise people to place items, and what do you suggest these items should be?

Loraine
St. Charles, MO

If you have the luxury of space in your dining room, there are many furniture pieces that you can consider. A buffet will give you a useful surface for serving, and will supply valuable storage for larger serving pieces. A dresser or hutch  will hold a display of china and crystal, and if space allows, a rolling serving tray can display silverware or other collectibles.

D

ear Michael,

My kitchen has an annex which would best be described as a breakfast nook, but I don't find anything nook-ish about it. It's really a room in its own right, just without walls and a door separating it. I'm not particularly keen on entertaining large groups, and would like to consider using this "nook" as a dining room for small groups of guests. I just have a small table for four or, at a squeeze, five. What would you do to this space to make it feel slightly more formal, and definitely more separate from the kitchen?

Yusailo
Hollywood, CA

More kitchens have counters with chairs these days. The breakfast nook may be a thing of the past as they take valuable real estate in a kitchen and, with the frantic pace of life, rarely get used as anything but a design element. If you have a nook that you never use, you should question whether the space would be better used for storage.

Begin by imagining there is a wall separating this room from the kitchen. I would consider your nook as a second dining room, albeit a small one, and treat it with the same formality as your main dining room. Purchase formal dining chairs  with arms, thereby immediately setting this space apart from the kitchen. If there are any architectural details defining the space that allow the walls to be painted a different color, then certainly do it. Use an area rug to further define the space and hang draperies to differentiate it from the kitchen's utilitarian nature. With art on the walls, decorative accessories on display, fine linen, crystal and silverware, even a cereal breakfast will feel like you're eating in a fine hotel.

D ear Michael,

I'm going to redo my house's dining room and want to avoid the formal cliche. I want it to be attractive, while being neither pretentious nor post-modern sparse. Can you give some tips on how to do this?

Pooky
New Brunswick, NJ

If you want your dining room to be beautiful, comfortable and elegant while being handsomely rich but unpretentious, look no further than contemporary high-end hotels for inspiration. The material used in these buildings are should give you a good template -- stone or wood floors, beautiful area rugs, fine fabrics on draperies and furniture. Note the absence of ornamentation, and also notice the colors are often neutrals on the walls with trims of white or off-white. The color comes from decorative accessories, rugs, art, and fresh flowers.

Dear Michael,

My house doesn't have a dining room, so we're planning on converting our living room (which we never use) into one. We have 4 kids, so we really need a comfortable place to sit. Since it's a living room, we will have a lot of extra space once the table is put in. What do you think we should do with it, especially around the fireplace?

Ian
Hartford, CT

Using your living room as a dining room is a good idea because the space lends itself to a large table, and you will still be able to use it for entertaining. I suggest you create a seating arrangement around the fireplace as if it were a living room. This will further homogenize the space into a mix between a dining room and a living room, and will also provide a visual separation between the table and fireplace. I do not recommend putting the table next to the fireplace because the chairs will obscure it from view when standing in many parts of the room. Also, you do not want your children to leave the table with toasted backs!

D ear Michael,

Our house has both a formal dining room and a dining room attached to the kitchen. We actually use the formal dining room nightly, and seem to only use the room for breakfast. We haven't done any decoration in this room, so it is most uninviting. I was hoping you could give us some tips for how to make our "breakfast room" a bit more attractive.

William and Isabelle
Portland, ME

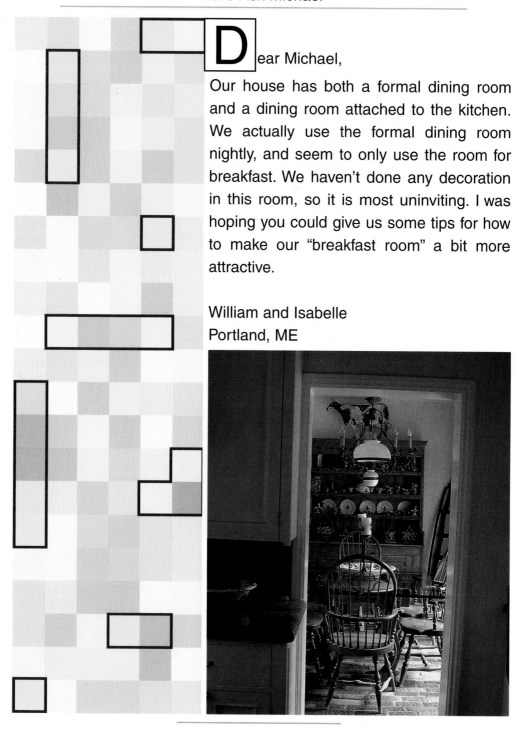

What could be more appropriate for day-to-day meals than a country breakfast room? There's something inviting about a totally casual, informal space for enjoying breakfast. The room pictured has French doors that fill the room with natural light. A pine Welsh dresser allows for display of decorative china and other farm-themed accessories, which further adds to the informality of the space. The glass table top allows the attractive heavy wood base to be seen, and the wood Windsor chairs complete the seating arrangement.

chapter 6

the family room

"Cozy." "Cushy." "Comfortable." "Inviting." "Warm." "Plush." "Informal." These are some of the most frequently uttered words when it comes to designing a family room. This is the room where you can throw formality aside, sit down with a remote control or book in hand, and sink into a couch en route to absolute relaxation. The family room should be distinctly yours, with personal pictures and collectibles abounding throughout the space.

Crucial to the modern family room is a television, along with the requisite throng of electronic peripherals. Some people opt to make these the center of attention by proudly displaying each on an individual shelf, while others conceal them behind cabinetry. The room should be tailored to the needs and wants of the users, so if an array of blinking lights screams "home" to you, then by all means display them!

Dear Michael,

We have a formal family room and my husband just bought a huge TV. That and all the other pieces of equipment look awful, and tremendously out of place in this otherwise formal room. I have seen you use pieces of custom furniture in your show to hide electronics, but I cannot recall a situation where you did it in a formal setting. Would an entertainment cabinet look out of place in a room like mine? I do not mind seeing the television or the equipment, I just want it to be presented in a classy way.

Paige and James
Buffalo, NY

You can definitely have an entertainment center cabinet in your formal family room. There are many pieces of furniture available that are designed to hold large televisions and the associated equipment. All the equipment can be in cabinets with doors, and drawers can provide storage for CD's and DVD's.

When I design cabinets, I like to integrate display spaces to show off a client's collectibles. In the piece pictured below, the owner used some of the free spaces for books and fine china pieces.

Before

After

Dear Michael,

I've heard you mention that men always want all white rooms. Obviously it's not wholly unsuccessful since so many get their way, and consequently there are a lot of all white rooms out there. Well I don't want a room all in white, but I do like the philosophy behind it. Can I do a room in all one color, like red, yellow, or purple? I think it would be great to walk into a space that is all one color, but I'm worried it will not look good. Do you have any advice on colors to use or examples of where I could see a completely monotone room?

Leigh
Boulder, CO

I once did a master bathroom where the client allowed me to use only one color -- white. Finding pure white marble slab for the vanity top and tile for the floor was very difficult. The white fixtures, faucets, towel bars, vanity, and so forth were easy.

I share your concerns about a single color overwhelming the senses, but I can imagine certain rooms where it might be successful. A home theater could be a single color like red because much of the time the room will have low lighting and the red will provide an intimate feel. You can go really wild with color in guest powder rooms because they are small

Photography by Santiago Irigoyen

spaces and no one spends much time in them. In fact, the small size of a guest powder room allows you to do things that would otherwise be far too expensive on a larger scale.

Small rooms are not, however, the only spaces that can be dominated by one color. The materials in the family room pictured above are exclusively purple. By using different shades, hues, and values, I managed to find a balance that was not overwhelming and allowed the room to take on a unique personality.

This combination of eight different fabrics, leathers, and carpets would all individually be considered purple, yet demonstrate the wide diversity possible within a color category. Notice how each works well with the others, showing that with care, you can have a full scheme working with only one general color.

D

ear Michael,

I recently moved into a typical 1970's house. This house is absolutely, positively, and resolutely boring! We bought it for its size and location, but not for its style.

We want to redo a room that will function as a living room/family room, so we need it to be comfortable for us yet formal for entertaining. I have a lot of Victorian furniture that has been in my family for years, so I need to know how to create a Victorian space. What are the essentials of Victorian style?

Jerry and Susan
Encino, CA

Redoing a 1970's house necessitates a lot of undoing before one can start doing. Many feature dated design elements that need to be removed before the redesigning can take place. Once they are gone, however, you have spaces that can be customized in nearly every conceivable way. 1970's builders favored inexpensive materials, so gutting the spaces is easier than in houses from other periods when quality materials were used.

The essentials of Victorian style are the complexity of design and ornate embellishments. Woods tend to be carved and dark, and fabrics are typically heavy with extensive use of trims. Start by eliminating the 1970's design elements, such as aluminum doors and windows, cottage cheese acoustic ceilings, and thick carpeting. Once these have been removed, consider adding door and window casings, base and crown mouldings, and a traditional mantle. Once the room is painted in a rich, vibrant color, you will be ready to add Victorian accessories, resulting in a room that is both comfortable and formal. (*Final product on next page*)

D

ear Michael,

We have been living in our house for about five years now, and while much of it looks good now, we still have one room that needs help. There's nothing in it at all! We are hoping to make it into a really cozy family room kind of space with a television cabinet, couches, and chairs. The space itself is not huge, but it is a good size at approximately 19' x 13'. One wall has small windows on it, and the rest of the space is essentially blank.

Can you give us some tips on how to make this room into a really cozy family room? We don't have kids yet, but when we do would like this to be the place where we spend a lot of time.

Lucerne and Bill
Nashua, NH

The Family Room

A family room, by definition, should be warm, inviting, and casual. It needs to be a place where you can be the real you with no pretensions, so it has to reflect your personality. I suggest a wall of cabinetry where you can display your favorite books, photos, collectibles, and souvenirs of your life. Such cabinetry can hold a television, its components, and a sound system. The seating should be particularly comfortable and practical. If you have hardwood floors, use an area rug to further warm the space. Ensure the room has warm lighting by using low wattage, warm

bulbs in typically "homey" fixtures, such as sconces, floor lamps, and table lamps. You should avoid using a ceiling pendant fixture, and only use recessed lighting if it is connected to a dimmer. Both of these lights typically carry a formal quality not needed in a family room. Window treatments, preferably in fabric, will finish the room.

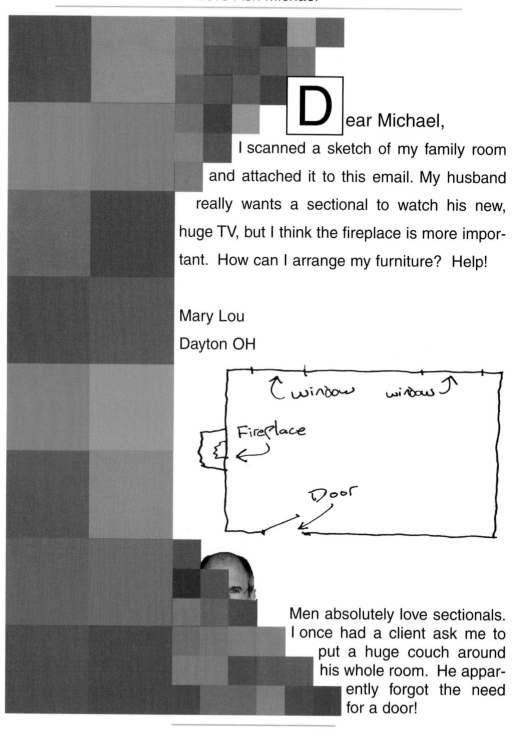

Dear Michael,

I scanned a sketch of my family room and attached it to this email. My husband really wants a sectional to watch his new, huge TV, but I think the fireplace is more important. How can I arrange my furniture? Help!

Mary Lou
Dayton OH

Men absolutely love sectionals. I once had a client ask me to put a huge couch around his whole room. He apparently forgot the need for a door!

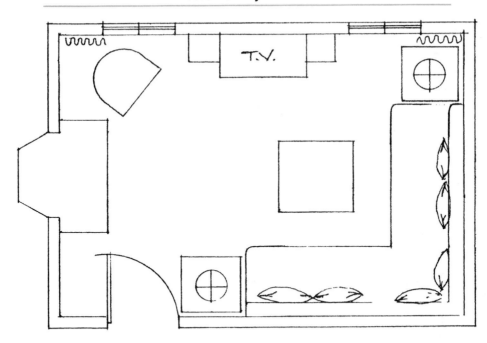

I believe a sectional will provide the best compromise between your husband's wish to watch television and your desire to easily view the fireplace. If you put the television between the two windows, then you should have a clear sight line to your fireplace from the east wall. Similarly, your husband will be able to sit on the south portion of the sectional and watch his television.

I recommend purchasing a square ottoman and placing it equidistant from the two arms of the sectional. Not only will it give both of you a place for your feet, but will also serve as a coffee table when used along with a tray.

Dear Michael,

My husband and I are color blind. Okay, that's sort of a lie, but after my mother just visited, I almost believe it. Apparently we just aren't very good at creating any kind of color scheme in our rooms.

We are about to redo our family room and we don't want to fall into the same trap as we have elsewhere in the house. The word my mother kept using, and I've heard you use on your show, is "cohesive." Can you explain what you mean by that so two color-blind people might have an attractive family room?

Jenni and Mike
Santa Cruz, CA

Work with a professional designer to choose a fabric you love, then let that designer take the guesswork out of the color picking process for the rest of the room. Closely study the fabric, match the colors with paint chips for picking a wall color, and coordinate other fabrics used in the room with it. With time and professional help, you can't fail!

The color scheme is carefully applied throughout this room. The rug, chairs, mirror frame, throw pillows, art above the fireplace, decorative plates, wood color, ottomans, and even jelly beans, all share a similar color scheme composed of yellows, purples, reds and blues.

To make a cohesive color scheme, I often work around one particular object, such as a favorite painting or fabric. Pick the colors and patterns in that object and apply them to the rest of your room. Make sure everything in the room works with it. In this room, the colors are based on the art above the fireplace.

Dear Michael,

We have a really basic question for you. You know when you're redoing a room, and you give the family everything they want, but then there's still space in a corner left over? What do you do with the empty space? As you can guess, we have a family room with a vacant corner that has us stumped.

Paulette and Jim
Las Cruces, NM

It is not particularly unusual to have such a space. I suggest you consider a small game table setup with four small scale chairs. This will be ideal for playing cards or board games. Otherwise, two smaller lounge chairs or bergeres with a little side table between creates an intimate seating group. This will be a space where guests sit during parties, you sit to read, or your family comes for a game, so it should be casual, comfortable, and welcoming. If you opt for a table, ensure that it has some form of centerpiece.

D
ear Michael,

I've noticed in many of your shows you use custom furniture instead of premade items available in stores. What is the advantage of going custom, when surely you could find pieces to fit nearly every space?

Denise
Allston, MA

I prefer designing custom furniture because I can get exactly what my client needs. Such furniture fits precisely, functions perfectly, and looks exactly how I envision it in my design mind. Often it does not cost any more because there are no middlemen (retail and distribution outlets) making a profit.

The custom entertainment cabinet pictured tied a family room together that carried a pyramid theme throughout, and would have been impossible to find in stores.

D
ear Michael,

I would like to bring the outside inside my house in terms of decoration and color, but I don't have time to go around watering a bunch of plants. Can you suggest a color and decoration scheme that will satisfy this, but will not be completely overwhelming? I don't want anything too cute like pictures of parrots and vines all over the walls.

Pierce
Yonkers, NY

Take a walk in your garden or local park, taking special note of the colors of nature. They are extraordinarily varied, and the greens alone exist in every shade imaginable. As nature inspires me, let it inspire you. I tend to use neutrals like warm beiges and yellow tones on walls in addition to sage greens. You can bring brighter colors into your home through fabrics on the furniture and draperies. Beautiful floral fabrics abound, and you can create a botanical paradise if you choose. The use of silk flowers, plants, and trees will further bring the outside in with minimal maintenance required on your part. Woods are ideal for the furniture pieces, but if you simply cannot stomach wood, use fabrics that approximate natural tones.

Art is another way to decorate with nature. There is such a plethora of magnificent paintings of the countryside, flora, and fauna, that you will surely be able to find one to match both your taste and color scheme. Botanical prints are also attractive, decorative accessories.

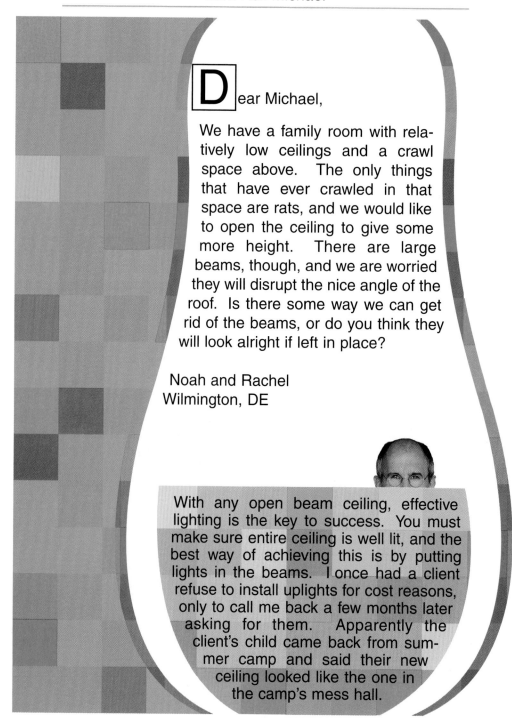

D ear Michael,

We have a family room with relatively low ceilings and a crawl space above. The only things that have ever crawled in that space are rats, and we would like to open the ceiling to give some more height. There are large beams, though, and we are worried they will disrupt the nice angle of the roof. Is there some way we can get rid of the beams, or do you think they will look alright if left in place?

Noah and Rachel
Wilmington, DE

With any open beam ceiling, effective lighting is the key to success. You must make sure entire ceiling is well lit, and the best way of achieving this is by putting lights in the beams. I once had a client refuse to install uplights for cost reasons, only to call me back a few months later asking for them. Apparently the client's child came back from summer camp and said their new ceiling looked like the one in the camp's mess hall.

I love the idea of opening up your family room ceiling. The change in the room's character will be dramatic. However, opening up the space is often easier said than done. Often electrical wiring and plumbing lines make the space most unattractive, and you may have walls that need to be relocated. Furthermore, it is unfinished so if the wood is unattractive it will have to be corrected. If you have beams, you will probably want to keep them not only for structural reasons but also because they can be made, through finishing and staining, to look extremely attractive. If the beams are diminutive, they can be boxed out to look more substantial, and uplights can be recessed in the top surface. If the underside of the roof is too unsightly, you can drywall it or use tongue and groove wood paneling. The latter solution is visually exciting whether it is stained or painted. All things considered, opening up the ceiling can be visually rewarding.

Dear Michael,

My husband and I bought a house with what was described as a "sun room." I don't know what it is and he's from Germany, so we don't really know what to do with this space. We do not have a proper family room, but instead the dining room and family room are merged. We would like to convert this sun room into a family room, but are far from convinced it's possible. It has high wood ceilings, sky lights, and large windows. Do you think a space like this can serve our purpose?

Helen and Stephen
Spartanburg, SC

There is no reason your sun room could not make an excellent family room, which by definition, is a comfortable place to relax, read, listen to music, and watch television. It is the latter which presents the challenge because of the need for light control. The best way to control light from the high skylight is with motorized blinds or screens. These can be translucent or opaque depending on your need to create complete dark-

ness. You will need drapery treatments for your many windows, which can be any style of shade or blind, both of which can be motorized as well. Your sun room can easily be transformed into a totally practical family room for use during the day and at night.

D

ear Michael,

I have acquired lots of pieces of furniture of every size and style. What do I do? I want a lovely home, not one that looks like a cluttered secondhand furniture store. My problem is now knowing what to keep and what to get rid of. There's a lot I like in this group, but most of it obviously doesn't work together well.

Ellen
Palm Springs, CA

photography by Bill Dow

You need to decide what stays and what goes. Keep only those pieces that you would choose to own if you were out looking for new furniture today, then start building the room around those pieces. The pieces can be quite dissimilar, but can work well together if united by a common style. In the photographs (*left and below*), the luxurious rolled arm sofa with its tailored flounce contrasts with the red leather, nailheaded straight backed sofa. The wing backed chairs flanking the fireplace work with the sofa as well. The drapery fabric and rug add another level of cohesion by uniting the colors of the upholstery.

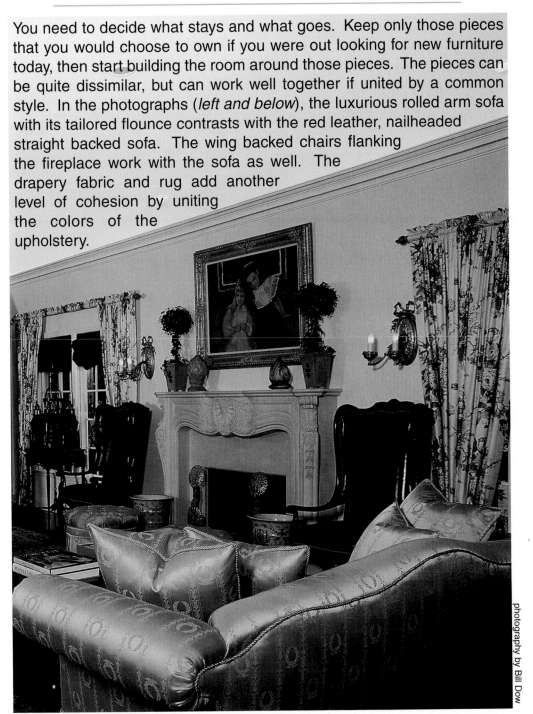

photography by Bill Dow

chapter 7

the rest of the house

The living room is cozy, the kitchen is personal, and the master bedroom is welcoming, but what should you do with that office? How should you go about making your kid a unique bedroom, and where should you start with the media room? There are rooms beyond the basic ones, and these need attention too in order to make a unified house, tailored to your desires.

The design challenges do not stop at the standard rooms, but the same methodology still applies when designing them. First, define your needs, and then take the room piece by piece. Pay attention to both the immediately obvious elements such as wall paint color and fabric upholstery, and also to the details that will reveal themselves upon closer inspection, such as the door knobs and cabinet lighting.

Never be afraid to personalize a room to your needs, even if seems to defy convention. If you want to put a small work desk in an entertainment room, there will certainly be a way to elegantly integrate the two. Your house should be exactly as you want it.

Dear Michael,

The last of our children just finished college and has moved out of our house. While my wife is busy lamenting our newly emptied nest, I'm looking to convert one of their rooms into a library.
The look I would ideally like is this: Imagine yourself standing inside of a wooden cube that has been hollowed out to become a room. I want the whole room to look as if it were carved from the same piece of wood, devoid of protruding cabinets and differing materials. Is this a look that will successfully translate from my imagination into reality? Also, is it possible to create enough storage space for both books and personal items using this look?

Wayne
West Hartford, CT

Photography by Bill Dow

Photography by Bill Dow

□ □ □

Your vision can absolutely become a reality so long as you have the funds and the services of a fine cabinet maker. The accompanying photographs show a fine example of what you describe. Your general concept is fabulous, but it is only in the details that it will truly shine. Only wood is visible inside this room because the walls are either wood shelves or paneling. The only exception is the fireplace which, by code, has to have a non-combustible material surrounding the firebox. The mantel, with corbels, is flanked on either side by exquisitely carved shell niches. The ceiling is coffered, which further gives the room a stature and richness from the gleaming wood. The hardwood floor has a decorative inlaid wood border that functions to further define the space. Completing the picture is the circular wood table with upholstered wood chairs. Note the small ladder (above), a wood-framed globe, leather reading chairs, and immaculately organized books and collectibles.

155

Dear Michael,

I am a busy stay-at-home working mom without a designated office space in our home. Currently I use our small guest bedroom (approximately 10' x 14') as my home office, but it is very uncomfortable and inefficient. What can we do to create an environment that feels less like a guest bedroom so that I can be comfortable during the day when doing office work, yet will function as a bedroom for my out-of-town in-laws (and grandparents) when they visit?

Selma

Mesa, AZ

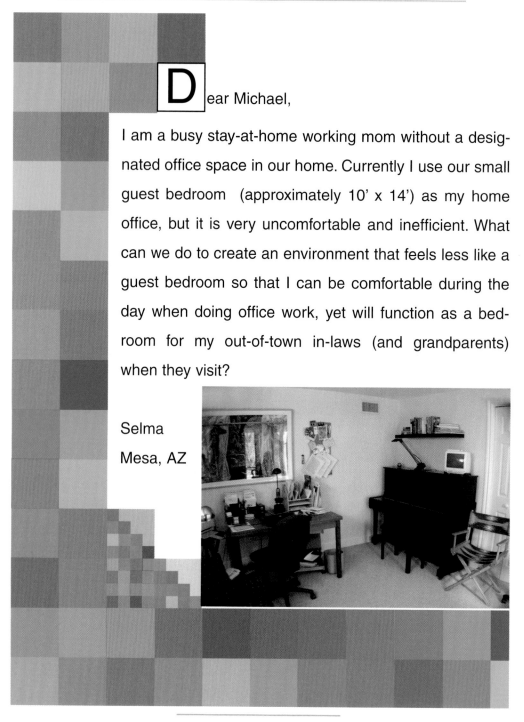

In the closed position, nobody would ever suspect a bed hides behind the rolling doors. Look closely and you can see a break in the center of the cabinetry where the doors slide to reveal the mattress.

Your situation is very typical. Often one room in a home needs to have a dual purpose. It sounds like a "Murphy" bed integrated with wall cabinetry could be a viable solution for your space because of the size of your room. When the bed is not in use, it can be housed vertically behind the cabinetry and the room will function as your office space. The cabinetry can have shelves and/or drawers for storage, books and display. When in the open position, the shelves slide to either side, thus creating your bedroom space.

Once opened, the room is converted into a bedroom. No personal items had to be moved, and the cabinetry design created nightstands on either side.

Dear Michael,

I have a bit of wall that I can't figure out what to do with that is in between two hallways. The only idea I've come up with is a display table, which is sort of boring. Can you think of anything more interesting?

Sofia
Dallas, TX

You might consider using that space to install a bar. Because of the nature of bars, you can make the counter nearly any shape you want just so long as a person can fit behind it. If you only have a minimal amount of wall space, then increase counter space by making it deeper. Even if you are not a keen entertainer, a bar can be a comfortable place to sit and talk, and it adds visual excitement to a space. Add comfortable charis to make it an inviting place to sit and relax, display attractive bottles and crystal, light the cabinets and counter, and the blank wall will come to life.

D

ear Michael,

I want to put a little desk in my entertainment room, but can't find the space. What should I get rid of -- one of the couches, the ottomans, the coffee table, or get a smaller entertainment cabinet?

Yoshihiro
San Francisco, CA

You will be pleased to hear that you might not need to remove any of the room's furniture. You could consider recessing the desk in a wall, which would give you a workspace without using too much floor space. Depending on your needs, the desk need not be much more than 30" deep and 36" wide. An attractive chair will fit nicely underneath it, and you will not have to sacrifice any of your entertainment room's seating.

If recessing the desk is not an option, I recommend removing one of the couches. The ottomans and table are almost certainly not in places the desk could go, so the couches are your only option.

D

ear Michael,

My husband gravitates toward simple color schemes and unornamented designs. I don't particularly mind this style, but I would like something completely different in my personal office. When I picture my ideal work space, I imagine myself working in a luxurious European palace. I love the attention to detail in those spaces, and the incredible complexity of colors and shapes. Have you ever designed a room in this style, and if so, could you give some pointers? Naturally, I do not have a queen's budget, but would like to feel like one in my office!

Antoinette
Boston, MA

Ornamentation and proper display of accessories are integral to the opulent look. While minimalism is common in modern high end design, the look requested by Antoinette is rooted in the castles and palaces harking back to medieval times. You must be careful to not clutter your space with too many items. Take a look at pictures of old English castles and you'll never see a table littered with too many personal items.

Creating the feeling of a palace involves more than having the grandeur of yesteryear, because implicit in creating such an environment is removing those elements that define the office of today. After the layout of your room is decided, it is time to focus on how to capture the opulence of the period. Cabinetry should be detailed, and doors and drawers should have interesting panels.

I once designed a home office (pictured below) in a very grand house, and had an artist paint an exquisite pattern in gold on the painted cabinets. Mouldings were highlighted with gold, adding a feeling of opulence, while avoiding the gaudy pitfalls gold poses. Because the ceilings of old homes are frequently coffered, I faux-painted the ceiling. The effect was dramatic. If you have blank walls, create panels, and either paint the inside of the panels or upholster them with fabric. Sconces are the best form of lighting for a palatial feel, and you must pay special attention to all hardware in the room.

Photography by Santiago Irigoyen

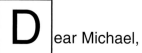

ear Michael,

My husband and I are expecting a child, and are planning on converting my office into the baby's room. We want to make our baby's room as different and special as possible, and avoid the cliched blue or pink color scheme (we don't know if we're having a boy or a girl yet!). Our problem is that we really don't know how to get out of the blue/pink trap!

Blaire and Kent
Las Vegas, NV

The baby's room prior to remodeling.

To make your baby's room as special as you want it, consider a graphic on the walls. You can hire an artist or you and your husband can have fun painting things which you think will amuse and delight your baby. Treat the walls and door as though they are one big canvas. Note even the window treatments fit into the mural above. Most of all, have fun!

The baby's room pictured depicts each major league baseball team through literal interpretations.

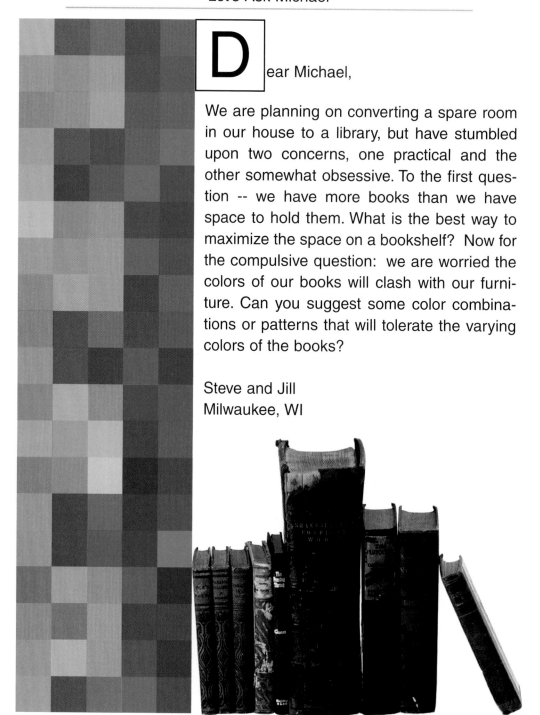

D

ear Michael,

We are planning on converting a spare room in our house to a library, but have stumbled upon two concerns, one practical and the other somewhat obsessive. To the first question -- we have more books than we have space to hold them. What is the best way to maximize the space on a bookshelf? Now for the compulsive question: we are worried the colors of our books will clash with our furniture. Can you suggest some color combinations or patterns that will tolerate the varying colors of the books?

Steve and Jill
Milwaukee, WI

To store and display many books, much thought needs to be spent in planning the room layout. Can all the furniture -- desk, chairs, sofas -- be situated away from any walls to allow book shelves to be built? Plan on having shelving sufficiently deep to accommodate the double stacking of books, as you will almost certainly grow your collection beyond your initial storage. Make your shelves adjustable, and keep like-sized books together. Keep the large, heavy books at the bottom of the cabinets so you do not stress the shelves, and also to add visual weight to the lower portion of the cabinets. Build your shelves to the ceiling and use a step stool or library ladder to reach the higher shelves.

Regarding your concern about books' color, do not dwell on the colors of the books. They will look lovely regardless of the colors of the furnishings. Books have a way of looking splendid wherever they are placed, and the visual confusion their various spine designs create is all part of the charm of having a library.

Photography by Christopher Covey

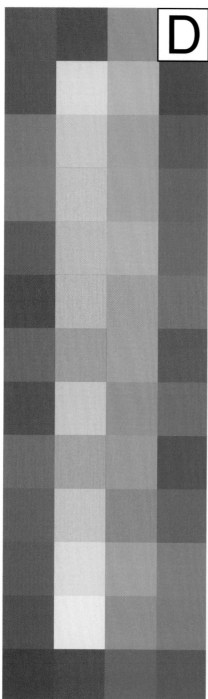

Dear Michael,

I just came back from a trip with my husband to South Africa and now am inspired to recreate the Serengeti. We are about to redo our home office and I would like to use this theme in the room. I want nature tones, animal prints, and and everything else that will remind me of the trip. My husband does not share my vision. He thinks animal prints are tacky and that we should redo our office in a conservative style. Can you help me with this debate?

Vanessa and Ben
Aurora, IL

There is ample room for compromise here. I can fully understand why your husband believes an office should be conservative, because nearly every office in our society adheres to a conservative ideal. I can also understand why you would want to recreate a lasting memory of your fabulous trip. As with most interior design dilemmas, you can have both.

Make the cabinetry throughout the room a richly stained wood and maximize the efficiency of the space. It can be less office-like by the use of cabinet pulls, and accessorized by native baskets for holding office supplies and waste. Animal prints can be used on the sofas, chairs, pillows and throws. If used sparingly, they will avoid appearing tacky. The walls of this room can be adorned with pictures of your trip or art reminiscent of the experience. Finally, find a beautiful animal-themed table to finish off the room. I have seen them in a variety of animal themes, such as lions, elephants, and monkeys.

Dear Michael,

We want to redo our son's room but don't have a lot of money for it. The room itself isn't missing much, in that he has a bed and an attached bathroom, but we feel like it isn't personal enough for his tastes. He goes over to his friends' houses and they all have these creative rooms! Can you give us any tips as to how we can make him feel like his room is specially made for him?

Caroline and Scott
Cazenovia, NY

A theme is a good starting point for personalizing your child's room. This client had a child who loved cars.

This is a very common request by parents of young children. Let's assume your son likes cars, as did the child whose room is pictured on this page. Very reasonably priced items were purchased in line with this theme, such as a bed shaped as a racecar that takes a standard size mattress, and bookcases that hold his collection of model cars and books. I created a gas pump by adding a top to a bookcase with a rope "hose" on the side. An area rug of a city with roads provided a perfect play space for models, and automotive posters and stickers adorned the walls. Auto accessories like new gas cans or clean engine parts from a junk yard completed room. Similar to this project, choose a theme that delights your son, and carry it throughout the room.

D ear Michael,

I want a classy office that will impress people who come visit me. I am tired of working with the IKEA desk (which has served me well!) that simply does not exude 'success.' Any tips you can give would be great. Thank goodness for email so I can ask you questions that I would otherwise be somewhat embarrassed about!

Tyler
North Hampton, MA

A change in room color to a deep, bold color achieves miracles. The most effective deep colors are blues, greens, and reds, and will be the first thing people notice upon entering the space. Obviously, the more money you are willing to spend, the higher quality furniture you can put in. Do not, however, underestimate the enhancing effects smaller, less expensive, items can have. Window treatments should be smart, but elegant, framed art should adorn the wall instead of calendars, and the office on a whole should be as organized as possible. If there is room for

furniture to display personal items, then do so. The personal touch makes an inviting and welcoming atmosphere for visitors and yourself.

ear Michael,

I've attached a hand drawn sketch to this email so that hopefully you can see what I try to describe. I know it's not up to your standards, but it's the best I could do!

As you can see, I have a long, wide hallway that attaches to my living room. There is a fireplace, a set of windows, and a grand piano in that room, so there really is not much space to put a bar. That is why I am writing to you -- I want a bar in this space, but I just can't figure out where to put it. I don't need it to be very large because I don't own much liquor, but it would be nice to have a place where a group of people could sit and talk over a drink. Can you see anywhere in this space to put such a thing?

Rob
Long Branch, NJ

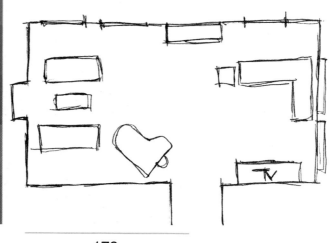

From your sketch, it appears you face a furniture piece on the opposite wall as you enter the living room from the hallway. I suggest you place the bar in the furniture's place. Because bars can be attractive pieces of design, I would make the bar the focal point as you walked down the hall. Putting the bar in the couch's position will also create a divider between your living room and the television area.

The bar pictured has a moved cherry face with a green granite counter, and is 36" high to accommodate low stools. As the room had an art deco, streamlined, modern look, great care was taken to choose stools that fit the room appropriately. Make sure you spend time on the details of your bar, such as the stools, to ensure thematic consistency.

Photography by Christopher Covey

Dear Michael,

I have a spare room that my father-in-law is pushing to become a library. He claims it will be a good place for my kids to learn the virtues of reading. I tend to agree with him, but I am worried I simply don't have sufficient books to fill the space. If I put shelves around the room I will have space for thousands of books. Well-read as I would like to think I am, I do not have nearly enough volumes to fill the space. What do you suggest I do with all the shelf space? Is there some sort of expandable shelving system I could invest in?

Chaime
Sioux Falls, SD

Home libraries often end up serving as supplementary living rooms. Because of the multitude of personal items, and the intimate feeling the high shelves provide, libraries can be an ideal location to entertain guests. If you do not have enough rooms to have both a living room and a library, consider creating a hybrid of the two.

I agree with the concept of the library as a quiet, peaceful retreat in which you can study and read. However, library shelves can certainly hold more than just books. I am confident there is a good chance there are collectors in your family, and what better place to show off these items? Intersperse the books with your favorite personal collectibles, your children's creations, photographs, and objet d'art. You will be amazed how quickly a room full of shelving will fill up with such items.

Your shelving system should be adjustable, and if you have insufficient items to display, remove a shelf or two until they are needed.

The owner of the library pictured below has a large collection of both books and pre-Columbian art. The library, with floor to ceiling cabinets, afforded the space to display both collections.

D ear Michael,

We have an entertainment room with a set of windows opposite the television cabinet that look directly into our neighbor's bedroom. While it is probably they who should be concerned about privacy, there is something strange about having our movies and television shows being readily viewable. With that said, we do not want to sacrifice the natural light that flows through these windows much of the day. Can you suggest a solution that will give us privacy while still allowing natural light to enter the space?

Gus and Susan
Frankfort, KY

There are several approaches to solving this problem. In fact it is more than just a privacy issue, as I suspect having the window reflecting on the television screen is bothersome when watching during the day. Adding a sheer drapery or translucent blind to the window will allow you to enjoy daylight while affording privacy. There could then be an overdrapery to completely cut out the light.

Another approach is to have a roman shade that closes *upwards*. This allows an uninterrupted view above when it is half closed, and privacy is given by the lower half. When total privacy is desired, and light control is required, it can be fully raised. This is particularly effective on smaller windows.

Shutters are a third alternative, as the vanes can be adjusted to provide privacy while still emitting light. However, shutters tend to remain closed, which would compromise the view.

The project shown on these pages illustrates the second approach, with upward closing roman shades. With the shades closed (*top*), little light enters the room, while in the bottom photograph light enters but privacy is preserved.

D|ear Michael,

You're going to think I live in a mansion, which I can assure you I don't. Anyway, I have a baby grand piano which I would like to dedicate a room to, but really have no feeling for what to do with the rest of the room. I've never seen this done before, so could you advise how you would go about decorating a dedicated piano room?

Buckley
Marina Del Ray, CA

The key to creating a successful piano room is to decide who the room is for -- you, the player, or the listener, or perhaps it is just for show. This determines the orientation of the piano. The lid of your baby grand is hinged on the straight side, typically away from your audience so sound is projected toward them. If, however, you want to enjoy a view from a nearby window as you play, the piano will be positioned accordingly. As far as the rest of the room is concerned, make sure there is comfortable seating and ample storage for associated musical paraphernalia.

The photograph shows a particularly lovely dedicated music room, with its black and white marble tile floor, seating for two, and beautiful decoration.

Photography by Bill Dow

178

Dear Michael,

My profession is that with words. Indeed, tis my job to spin these marvels of our wondrous species into stories, into entertainment, and most of all, hopefully into lessons. I need little more than an inkwell and parchment to accomplish this lofty, yet simple profession... mind and talent notwithstanding. Of late, I find myself needing more. I need space, Michael, I need places surrounding my desk to place the incidentals of modern life. And because I do not win the bread, per se, but more so does The Muse, I need music. And music, though a resident of air, is brought through cumbersome objects that require space as well. Please, good designer, help me with my space troubles.

Bianciccio
Portland, OR

I need to begin by complementing you on what is hands down the most amusing email I have received. The answer to your needs lies in nicely designed cabinetry. This will include a writing surface for quill or computer, with all the necessary storage space for inks, parchment, and files. In essence, a desk. But beyond that, you need cabinetry to hold yours and others' writings, and your source of music. Your complete sound system can be on the shelves within easy reach, and the speakers can also be housed there. The shelving will accommodate your collection of CDs or vinyl albums (I suspect you own the latter). A small television could also be installed if the need presents itself. With an artful design you will be able to create a working environment so conducive to fine writing that the impatient world awaiting your next masterpiece should not expect a lengthy delay. Write on!

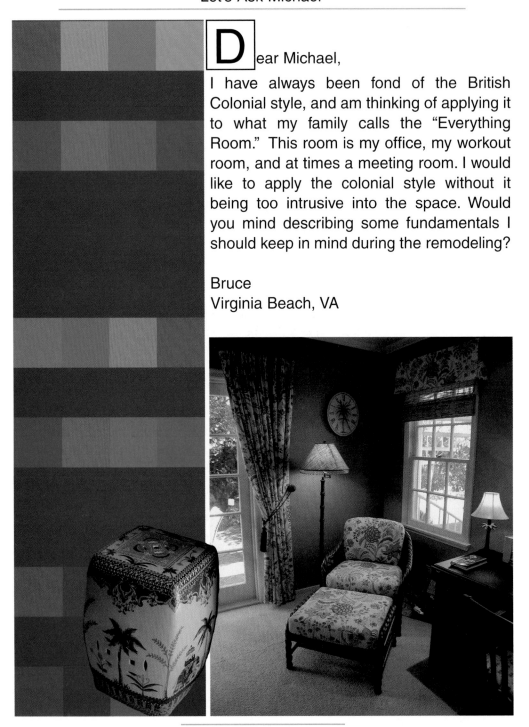

Dear Michael,

I have always been fond of the British Colonial style, and am thinking of applying it to what my family calls the "Everything Room." This room is my office, my workout room, and at times a meeting room. I would like to apply the colonial style without it being too intrusive into the space. Would you mind describing some fundamentals I should keep in mind during the remodeling?

Bruce
Virginia Beach, VA

The colonial styles harken back to those days in the 19th Century when Britain was busy trying to colonize the world. This included India, where they succeeded. The British took their then current homeland styles and re-interpreted them using local materials and incorporating local stylistic motifs. Dark wood tones predominate, and fabrics tend to be rich in color and pattern. Today's British Colonial tends to feature lots of rattan in addition to rich mahogany furniture.

In the photographs on this page, I chose a window shade made of bamboo which exudes a natural feeling appropriate to the tropical lands being colonized. In keeping with this theme, palm trees adorn the fabrics, decorative accessories, and art. Note the palm tree table lamp and the bamboo floor lamp. When bold wall colors are used, British Colonial rooms exude a rich, comfortable opulence... perfect for an "Everything Room!"

Pictured below is a staircase with large paintings in substantial frames hung at such a height as to be comfortably seen when standing in front, and distanced laterally so as to not compete with adjacent paintings.

ear Michael,

I have a staircase that is much like most staircases in that it both goes up and it has a large wall accompanying it. I feel as if hanging art on this wall is impossible because they will be arranged on the diagonal. How do you suggest I decorate the giant staircase wall?

Ash
Huntington, WV

The staircase wall presents a challenge and an opportunity. The large space allows large art pieces to be mounted, which can include tapestries, area rugs, quilts, large paintings, and sculptural pieces. I have even seen farm implements mounted on such a wall in a country home. If you have only smaller art pieces, either make a large, organized arrangement, or leave the wall blank. Placing small pieces in an unclustered form will cause them to be dwarfed by the space.

Photography by Bill Dow

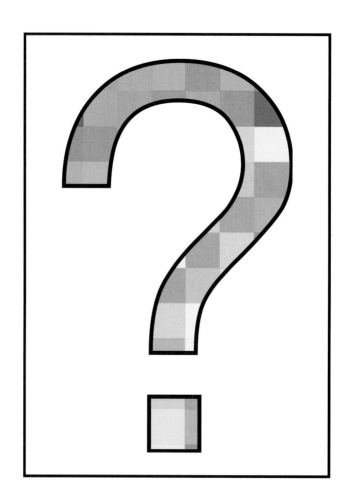

Appendix A

professional interior design

In the interest of truly answering all the questions I am most frequently asked, this appendix provides answers to questions about professional interior design. How can you become a professional interior designer? Where can you find one in your local area? What should you look for when hiring a professional designer? While you may have some ideas about how you can make a room both plush and utilitarian, you may need a professional designer to help translate your ideal into reality.

ear Michael,

My husband and I really enjoy watching *Designing For the Sexes* every week and we both always love your final product... this being true even when a room is not done in our particular style.

We live in the Dallas area and purchased a new home this year. It is not decorated yet as we want to do everything "just right" and with the help of an interior designer. We always talk about how we would love to hire you to help us out but I'm sure that is out of the question. Hence, I am writing you this email in hopes of you being able to advise us on how to hire an interior designer and in hopes of the possibility of you possibly referring someone to us. I'm not really sure if it is you, Michael Payne, reading this email but I thought it might be worth a try to send it to you.

Dina
Dallas, TX

I do not personally know any designers in the Dallas area, but suggest you contact the local chapter of the American Society of Interior Designers (ASID) and explain to them what you are looking for in a designer. Ask them for three or four referrals and interview each of them. Aside from the project, be sure to discuss fee structures because designers do charge differently. Ask the potential designers for references of past clients and definitely contact these references to understand more about the designer. Choose the one with whom you feel most comfortable and who you think best understands what you want. Remember that interior design is not about what the designer wants to do, but about how the designer can give you what you want. Avoid any designers who wants to force their taste on you.

ear Michael,

I've watched your show since it first came on and have decided I want to become an interior designer. Where do I even begin doing this? What schooling is necessary, and what education did you have to get to be where you are? Also, just out of curiosity, do you have any acting experience?

Deirdre
Rutland, VT

I am delighted to hear you have chosen to pursue a career in interior design! It is necessary to have an education in the field because, as a professional designer, you will be expected to have a broad knowledge on many subjects. You will need to learn the language of design, learn to draft, understand structure, and learn fundamental dimensions and codes for residential and commercial projects. This will enable you to communicate with other professionals as well as government officials if you need to apply for permits.

There are a number of schools offering excellent interior design programs. It is important you enroll in a FIDER accredited program. This will guarantee you of a first class education and provide the requirements for admittance to a professional organization such as ASID (American Society of Interior Designers).

I went through the Interior Design Program at UCLA and worked at a design firm for four years before starting out on my own. My television show came much later. As for acting experience, I have absolutely none, and I am exactly the same person in reality as you see on the show... it's reality television at its truest!

189

Dear Michael,

You have talked a lot about having custom furniture made, and I am wondering about some of the logistics of this. Where do you find someone to make it? What do you have to give to the manufacturer? Do you need to have some sort of license to design furniture? Also, how much more expensive is it to have something custom made than to just buy it in the store?

Oliver
Macon, GA

The logistics of having custom furniture made are very straightforward. You need to be able to express your needs in a sketch or drawing to scale so the manufacturer can clearly understand your requirements. The drawing will show the width, height, and depth, and a photograph can show style and detail if you cannot draw these aspects. And how do you find this manufacturer? The yellow pages should have a "Furniture -- Custom-Made" section, and if not, try "Cabinet Makers."

Custom-made furniture is often not more expensive than buying retail because the middleman has been eliminated. However, even if it is more expensive, you will benefit by having a piece exactly as you want it. It will be tailored to your exact needs, which is worth a lot.

D|ear Michael,

My wife and I are considering purchasing a relatively old house (by U.S. standards). We don't have an exact date, but were told that it was "pre-1930." In your experience, is this a safe thing to do, and should we be on the look out for any particular problem areas?

Alex and Veronica
Los Angeles, CA

I am always amused when I hear a home described as "old." Pre-1930's houses are considered old by American standards, but are relatively new by British standards. I would be wary of old homes, and suggest thoroughly investigating the house's infrastructure, including the plumbing, electrical, and heating systems. Often  these systems are of borderline functionality and safety. Plumbing leaks may have rotted wooden structural members, electrical wiring may be inadequate for contemporary loads, and heating systems might use asbestos in the ducting. Upgrade these upon purchase of an old house so all the beautiful redesign and decoration will not have to be disturbed down the road. Do not be discouraged by the need to upgrade. Older homes have character and often possess beautiful architectural details that would cost a fortune to reproduce today.

INDEX